Sherman Studies of Judaism in Modern Times
General editor: John R. Hinnells

JEWISH–CHRISTIAN RELATIONS
SINCE THE SECOND WORLD WAR

To Devorah

GEOFFREY WIGODER

Jewish–Christian relations since the Second World War

Manchester University Press ⏻

Manchester and New York

Distributed exclusively in the USA and Canada
by St. Martin's Press, New York

Copyright © Modern Jewish Studies Fund and Geoffrey Wigoder 1988

Published by Manchester University Press
Oxford Road, Manchester M13 9PL, UK

Distributed exclusively in the USA and Canada
by St. Martin's Press, Inc., 175 Fifth Avenue, New York, NY 10010, USA

British Library cataloguing in publication data
Wigoder, Geoffrey
 Jewish–Christian relations since the Second World War.
 1. Christianity and other religions—Judaism—1945-
 2. Judaism—Relations—Christianity—1945-
 I. Title II. Series
 261.2'6   BM535

Library of Congress cataloging in publication data
Wigoder, Geoffrey
Jewish–Christian relations since the Second World War / by
Geoffrey Wigoder.
  p.   cm.
Bibliography: p. 168
Includes index.
ISBN 0-7190-2639-3: $30.00 (est.)
1. Judaism—Relations—Christianity—1945-
2. Christianity and other religions—Judaism—1945-   I. Title
BM535.W485 1988
296.3'872—dc 19

ISBN 0-7190-2639-3

Typeset in Guardi
by Koinonia Limited, Manchester
Printed and bound in Great Britain by
Anchor Brendon Ltd, Tiptree, Essex

BM
535
. W485
1988

CONTENTS

FOREWORD

This book is based on a series of lectures given in the University of Manchester's Department of Comparative Religion, inaugurating the Sherman visiting lectureship on Modern Jewish Studies endowed by the Sherman Trusts.

The subject was chosen both because of its appositeness and because of my own interests and involvement. The positive achievements in the field of Christian–Jewish relations within a few decades have been remarkable. As a student I had the privilege of attending the very first international conference of Christians and Jews, which was held in Oxford in 1946. Subsequent progress has greatly exceeded the comparatively modest expectations of those then gathered. At the same time, many problematic areas remain. I have endeavoured to describe both the accomplishments and the continuing obstacles.

'Christian' and 'Jewish' views on the subject are each so complex because of the variety of viewpoints on either side that one could be stymied at the outset if one sought scientifically-based consensuses. Norms cannot be defined nor 'heresies' determined in the area we are about to examine. Religions are composed of interweaving standards and even inner contradictions. It has been said that every age has its pre-modernists, modernists and post-modernists living side by side, and our age is no exception. Many different Church groups have issued post-war statements concerning Jews and a plethora of theologians have addressed themselves to the subject. Selectivity is inevitable in quoting from the Church statements or citing individual thinkers, but it is hoped that the general lines portrayed are as representative as possible.

I would like to express my gratitude to Professor John Hinnells, Head of the Department of Comparative Religion at the University of Manchester, for his personal initiative in establishing this visiting lectureship, for his invitation and friendship. It is to be hoped that his goal of establishing a permanent lectureship in Jewish Studies at the University will soon be crowned with success.

G.W.

GENERAL INTRODUCTION

In an effort to facilitate a greater understanding of Judaism as a *living* religion, the Department of Comparative Religion at Manchester University is seeking funding for a full-time lectureship on 'Judaism in modern times'. As a result of funds donated mainly by the Sherman Trusts but also by Marks and Spencer, the first series of Sherman Lectures was held in February 1987. These four public lectures are a first step on a longer path and in a larger project. The focus of these and subsequent lectures is the study of Jews and Judaism in the nineteenth and twentieth centuries. The perspective will vary in each series, encompassing not only religion, history and philosophy, but also sociology, politics and the arts. Jewish communities in various parts of the world, Israel, Britain, America and elsewhere, will be included.

Perhaps no religion has suffered such consistent misrepresentation as Judaism has experienced in the Christian West. Anti-Semitism has become intertwined in Christian teaching and practice. Judaism has been characterised as legalistic and dictionaries continue to equate 'Jew' with 'cheat'. All too often in courses on Christianity Judaism is presented as dying, becoming redundant or fossilised after the birth of Jesus. Books rarely refer to the centuries of persecution of Jews at the hands of Christians and the Christian world was deafeningly silent at the Holocaust, with the Church protesting only over the fate of Jews who had converted to Christianity. Little attention is paid to the plethora of Jewish contributions in the modern world in philosophy, law, medicine, music, psychology and so on. A number of Jewish thinkers would argue that anti-Jewishness is inherent in the Christian Gospels; doubtless it can be seen in the writings of some so-called liberal modern theologians. The prejudice is not always self-conscious, but it is no less dangerous for that. Compounded with all this, many Jews suspect, is the possibility that nations and peoples are antagonistic to the State of Israel for political reasons in an oil-dependent world.

Yet the last forty years have seen substantial shifts of perspective. Understandings have developed on both sides which could hardly have been imagined at the turn of the century. The horror of the Holocaust has traumatised some and changed many, resulting in both the hardening and softening of attitudes. This book, written by an active participant in the Jewish–Christian dialogue, faces some hard questions and does not flinch from frank answers, nor is it timid in its reflections on controversial issues. Without doubt it will challenge and provoke many. The book is both about and part of the lively Jewish–Christian debate. Geoffrey Wigoder, as Director of the Oral History Institute in Jerusalem, and as joint editor of *The Encyclopedia Judaica*, is outstandingly well qualified to write on Jewish–Christian relations since the Second World War. His Sherman Lectures launched our Manchester project with vigour, intellectual challenge and personal warmth. There can be little doubt that this book will provide equal stimulus to an international readership.

John R. Hinnells
Professor of Comparative Religion,
University of Manchester

CHAPTER 1

Christian attitudes to Judaism and the Jews

Our survey is to cover less than half a century, within the lifetime of many, a short period which has witnessed a revolution in major aspects of the Christian–Jewish relationship. In his epoch-making book, *The Conflict of the Church and the Synagogue*, one of the great pioneers of that revolution, the English scholar James Parkes, could write in 1934:

> The Christian public as a whole, the great and overwhelming majority of the hundreds of millions of nominal Christians in the world, still believe that the Jews killed Jesus, that they are a people rejected by their God, that all the beauty of the Bible belongs to the Christian Church and not to those by whom it was written; and if on this ground, so carefully prepared, modern anti-Semites have reared a structure of racial and economic propaganda, the final responsibility still rests with those who prepared this soil and created the deformation of the people.[1]

In other words, the anti-Jewish and anti-Judaistic teachings and practices of Christendom, stretching back to the Church Fathers and the first Christian rulers of the Byzantine Empire, still in the 1930s remained current and unchallenged among most Christians. Of course in many parts of the world, especially in the West, the consequences of Enlightenment had brought the Jew out of the ghetto and granted him full civil rights, but that had not affected theological attitudes. The Churches and their theologians continued to expound the same negative doctrines and stereotypes. Exceptions could be cited in some Protestant Churches where even a certain philo-Semitism came to expression. But as an illustration of the speed of the mills of God, it could be noted that only in 1986 did the House of Bishops of the Church of England issue instructions to exclude from the Holy Week liturgy prayers that could be regarded as anti-Semitic (and then only on the initiative of the Bishop of Birmingham, himself of Jewish origin).[2]

A few voices heard before the Second World War did indeed foreshadow later trends. Parkes himself cited one predecessor, Conrad Moehlman of the Colgate-Rochester Divinity School, author in 1933 of *The Christian–Jewish Tragedy: A Study in Religious Prejudice*. Parkes called it 'too emotional to be convincing' but noted that it did teach that the charge of deicide rested on false accounts in the New Testament.[3] Another pioneer work from the same year was Erik Peterson's *Die Kirche aus Juden und Heiden* which tried to present the Jews in a positive light from the standpoint of Christianity. Paul Tillich published a book in Germany, also in 1933, directed against Nazism, in which he found in the Hebrew prophets a political eschatology which could save Germany and the world from the barbarism of the Nazi movement. During the war, he broadcast to Germany from the United States, insisting that the Protestant faith was of Jewish origin, that the accusation of Jewish responsibility for the death of Jesus was an absurdity and that an attack on Judaism was a surrender of Christianity.[4] Another strong and influential voice being heard in the 1930s was that of Reinhold Niebuhr in the United States with his attacks on anti-Semitism and pleas for the abandonment of Christian triumphalism, while in France Jacques Maritain was writing: 'Israel is a mystery of the same order as the mystery of the world or the mystery of the Church. Like them it lies at the heart of Redemption' – although he could also write that the mystical body of Israel is an unfaithful and repudiated Church.[5] In England James Parkes set out to study anti-Semitism, which brought him to the study of Jewish history, and further to the study of Judaism. His conclusion was that Christianity based its theology of the Jews on bad history.

But these were lonely voices. Around the same time another theologian was writing: 'The Church of Christ has never lost sight of the thought that the "Chosen People" who nailed the redeemer of the world to the cross must bear the curse for its action through a long history of suffering . The final return of the people of Israel can only take place through the conversion of Israel to Christ.'[6] The writer was Dietrich Bonhoeffer (who never ceased to see the Jews as accursed, although he was to suppress such sentiments during the war when he expressed his identification with Jewish suffering).

Or to quote a sermon preached in 1937 on the Tenth Sunday after Trinity: 'The gospel lesson for the day throws light upon the dark and sinister history of this people that can neither live nor die because it is under a curse which forbids it to do either. Until the end of its days, the Jewish people must go its way under the burden which Jesus' decree has laid upon it.'[7] The preacher was Pastor Niemöller.

True, these voices came from inside Nazi Germany – albeit from theologians noted for their opposition to the regime – but similar quotations could be given from Christian sources, Catholic and Protestant, in many parts of the world for whom such sentiments were their stock-in-trade.

Organisationally, the first National Conference of Christians and Jews had been established in the United States in 1927.[8] Its object was the common fight against prejudice, especially anti-Catholicism, rather than what has become to be known as 'dialogue'. It sought common elements, especially in social issues, but did not study differences. The British Council of Christians and Jews came into existence during the Second World War with a similar anti-prejudice motivation. The very first international gathering of Christians and Jews was held in Oxford in 1946. The subject chosen was 'Faith, Responsibility, Justice', and a noble joint document was agreed upon, including a denunciation of anti-Semitism. It was a moving occasion (I was privileged to attend as the representative of British Jewish students) and the participants included three outstanding survivors from German concentration camps – the anti-Nazi pastors Grüber and Maas and Rabbi Leo Baeck. But the conference did not deal with the two issues that were to become paramount in Jewish–Christian relations in the post-war world: the role of Christian teaching in creating an atmosphere in which a Holocaust was possible – this realisation had not yet dawned – and the struggle for the Jewish State then in full swing (this would have split the conference, Jews and Christians alike, into Zionists and anti-Zionists).

But only a year later, at a further conference at Seeligsberg in Switzerland of what was now the International Council of Christians and Jews, a ten-point document was drawn up which was to have a historic impact. A major influence here was the French scholar, Jules Isaac, who while hiding from the Germans during the war had turned his attention to the study of Christian sources of anti-Semitism. Anti-Semitism was the prime concern of this conference (which was a meeting of individuals and enjoyed no support from Church hierarchies). The pioneering 'Ten Points of Seeligsberg' were to become the staple of dialogue. They were:

1 Remember that One God speaks to us all through the Old and the New Testaments.

2 Remember that Jesus was born of a Jewish mother of the seed of David and the people of Israel, and that His everlasting love and forgiveness embrace his own people and the whole world.

3 Remember that the first disciples, the apostles and the first martyrs were Jews.

4 Remember that the fundamental commandment of Christianity, to love God and one's neighbour, proclaimed already in the Old Testament and confirmed by Jesus, is binding upon both Christians and Jews in all human relationship, without any exception.

5 Avoid distorting or misrepresenting biblical or post-biblical Judaism with the object of extolling Christianity.

6 Avoid using the word 'Jews' in the exclusive sense of the enemies of Jesus, and the words 'The Enemies of Jesus' to designate the whole Jewish people.

7 Avoid presenting the Passion in such a way as to bring the odium of the killing of Jesus upon all Jews or upon Jews alone. It was only a section of the Jews in Jerusalem who demanded the death of Jesus, and the Christian message has always been that it was the sins of mankind which were exemplified by those Jews and the sins in which all men share that brought Christ to the Cross.

8 Avoid referring to the scriptural curses, or the cry of the raging mob, 'His blood be upon us and our children', without remembering that this cry should not count against the infinitely more weighty words of our Lord: 'Forgive them for they know not what they do.'

9 Avoid promoting the superstitious notion that the Jewish people are reprobate, accursed, reserved for a destiny of suffering.

10 Avoid speaking of the Jews as if the first members of the Church had not been Jews.[9]

(Although the conference was of Christians and Jews, the document was put out by the Christian participants.)

Only at this time, as the full horror and implications of the Holocaust dawned, did Christians begin a serious revision of their thinking concerning Jews, and this process was gradual. It was not until 1965, with the Vatican Council declaration, that there was to be another document of substance in the same spirit. The First Assembly of the Protestant World Council of Churches, meeting in Amsterdam in 1948, produced a document on the Christian Approach to the Jews, roundly condemning anti-Semitism, which by now was being denounced by many Churches. But the rest of the WCC statement proved highly unsatisfactory to Jews. After describing the unique position and contribution of Israel in the design of God, it stated: 'The Church has received this spiritual heritage from Israel and is therefore in honour bound to render it back in the light of the Cross. We have therefore to proclaim to the Jews "The Messiah for whom you wait has come. The promise has been fulfilled by the coming of Jesus Christ".' It proceeded to lay down that the Churches must consider mission to the Jews as a normal part of parish work. The recently-established State of Israel was mentioned – as a factor which would complicate anti-Semitism![10]

Fortunately elsewhere other themes began to obtrude. In 1953 Tillich propounded a programme to review Church publications to purge them of dangerous anti-Jewish stereotypes; to emphasise the Old Testament in the Church; to abandon any missionary movement to the Jews; to foster theological dialogue and joint activities in the struggle for social justice; and to accept the continuity and authenticity of the Jewish faith.[11] In the 1950s, Protestant churches and thinkers began to wrestle with the problems of Christian anti-Semitism, Jewish survival and self-identity, of the Old and New Testaments, of mission and of God's role in history. New biblical scholarship opened up fresh perspectives, as did the development of genuine interfaith dialogues. A parallel movement in the Catholic Church commenced in the early 1960s at the urging of Pope John XXIII. The framework was much broader than the Christian–Jewish relationship. A new liberalism in all theological attitudes combined with a puncturing of triumphalism in a growingly non-Christian world forced the rethinking of hoary traditions and doctrines, and the emergence of new viewpoints that would have been inconceivable not long before.

After this chronological introduction reviewing revisions in Christian thinking concerning Jews and Judaism since the war, I want now to examine some key themes. I will note not only the new positive directions but also the stubborn retention of traditional prejudices and the conservative voices still to be heard in various Churches. Outside the survey will be the Orthodox churches which have remained unaffected by liberalising trends, still ensconced in a medieval world. This would seem to apply to their theology and practices in general; it certainly is the case with regard to their attitudes to Judaism and Jews, with all the traditional negative stereotypes remaining enshrined in their liturgy and teachings. They continue to regard the 1965 Vatican Declaration on the Jews a betrayal of Christian doctrine.

But first let us hear a recent and positive voice projecting the essentials of a contemporary Christian theology of Judaism. The Swiss Catholic theologian, Clemens Thoma, has written:

> A Christian theology of Judaism must be aware of the complex character of Judaism, which is not readily categorised, of the danger of thinking in clichés and of past apologetic and polemically contorted discussions between Jews and Christians. Even the most fundamental alternatives do not admit of an easy and superficial answer. For example, were Jews after the death of Christ dismissed from the history of revelation or are they now as ever the people

of God? Can we accept theologically mutual influences or must we move into isolation again? Should we aspire to an intra-Christian ecumenical theology with or without the inclusion of Judaism? A Christian theology of Judaism would be nipped in the bud were we not to understand the Jews of our time, in one way or another, as people of God, were we not to rate very highly the Jewish character of Christianity and the Christian character of Judaism, and were we not to extend Christian *oekumene* to include Judaism (without a provocative mission to Jews).[12]

Already in this introductory passage, we meet many of the themes that are to concern us.

The 'Old' Testament

Among Christian theologians, there are still to be found those who continue to date the roots of the rejection of the Jews in the times of the so-called Old Testament. After the Vatican statements on Judaism, it has become difficult for Catholics to express such extreme views. The prominent proponents are Protestants, mostly German, who see the Jews as having betrayed the covenant already in the period following the Babylonian Exile, so that already then the true faith of ancient Israel was broken and 'Israel' declined to 'Judaism'. Thus the Bible scholar, Martin Noth, feels that the covenant with Israel ended in 586 BC with the destruction of the First Temple, as Israel had not maintained its loyalty. This was decisively confirmed with the destruction of the Second Temple and the loss of independence in AD 70. 'Israel thereby ceased to exist and the history of Israel came to an end. There was nothing but the Diaspora'(1958)[13] Similar viewpoints have been expressed by the New Testament scholars Martin Dibelius, Rudolf Bultmann and many others. They are derived from classical Christian theology and we should not let ourselves be deluded into thinking that new understandings have led to their disappearance.

However, other Christian scholars have reacted differently. In the words of André Lecocque of Chicago Theological Seminary:

The Christian Church has historically both deeply revered the

Jewish scriptures and felt deeply embarrassed by them. It has both paid tribute to the people of the Bible and stolen from them their sacred testimony, their soul. Christ has swallowed all of the Scripture and all of history. He so much fills the horizon that there is place left for no-one and nothing else. Christ becomes the *spirit* of Scripture while the Old Testament is merely its flesh.[14]

The Hebrew Bible then both unites and divides Jews and Christians. Both view the text anachronistically – the Jew through the spectacles of rabbinic tradition, the Christian through the prism of the New Testament and Christian hermeneutics and exegesis. In many churches, Christians have known only those sections used for Christological interpretation and these were the passages chosen for liturgical readings.

However, thanks to the insights of modern Bible scholarship, both Christian and Jewish, recent decades have seen a return to the original meaning and significance of the Old Testament. It was an innovation of the Vatican Council's *Nostra Aetate* Declaration in 1965 to say: 'The Church of Christ acknowledges that the beginnings of her faith and election are already found among the patriarchs, Moses and the prophets. The Church cannot forget that she received the revelation of the Old Testament through the people with whom God designed to establish the ancient covenant.'[15] It is not however to be expected that the fundamental thrust of Christian interpretation will be dropped. Thus, the fine 1973 document of the Committee for Catholic–Jewish Relations set up by French Catholic bishops, after stating that Christians must understand the Jewish tradition, must study the whole Bible and that the first covenant was not invalidated by the latter, continues: 'It is true that the Old Testament renders its meaning to us only in the light of the New Testament', adding 'but we must receive it and understand it by itself.'[16] A new recognition of the Old Testament can be found in statements from many other Churches although Protestants have had a long tradition of Old Testament study and understanding.

Great strides have been made in recent decades in the teaching of the Old Testament, both in the approach and the extent – to the chagrin of certain Arab Christian circles who would prefer that the Old Testament remain relegated and ignored because of its exposition of the link between the People of Israel and the Land of Israel. However, much of the attention paid to the Old Testament remains for its perceived prefiguration of Jesus and not for its own sake. In a Catholic context we shall see this when we consider the most recent Vatican document on the Jews (see p. 91) while for a Protestant attitude I cite the 1968 statement of the Faith and Order Commission of the World Council of Churches: 'The Old Testament shows Israel as an imperfect witness.'[17] Similarly the World Council of Churches' 1974 report on its Consultation on Biblical Interpretation and the Middle East states that the Old Testament is to be read and understood, interpreted and applied in the light of the New Testament, although it adds that there must be a careful reading and understanding of the text in its plain meaning, in its historical and literary context, and in the light of modern scientific knowledge of the original language of the Bible.[18]

However, new voices are being heard. The Catholic, Cornelius Rijk, wrote that the biblical renewal in Christian thinking is of the utmost importance and the theology is becoming more biblical. Christians are still struggling with the Old Testament which is seen as the preparation for the New Testament. To Rijk the *whole* Bible is gospel – good news – because the whole Bible throws the light of God's spirit on human history, revealing God and the covenant relationship.[19] The Vatican Council, he said, expressed the idea of cosmic revelation – itself a biblical concept – with God as the father and creator of all men, and *all* men are called on to collaborate with God in ongoing creation. Or, as simply put by the Vatican 'Guidelines' of 1974, 'The same God speaks in the Old Testament and the New Testament.'[20] In the word of the American Catholic, Eugene Fisher, 'Stripped of its basis in the Hebrew Scriptures, the New Testament makes little sense',[21] for which he gives a number of telling examples. However, Catholics have still far to go to recognise the Hebrew Bible as an authentic, *independent* religious document.

Among Protestant scholars, Markus Barth has written:

> Every page of the New Testament has a quotation or concept from

the Old Testament – not merely as timeless symbols or apologetic proof from prophecy but because they saw their good news as the continuation and coronation of God's history with Israel. The Old Testament is cited in the New Testament as an invitation to listen to the dialogue between God and Israel – and to join in it.[22]

The American Anglican theologian, Paul Van Buren, makes the simple assertion: 'The Old Testament reminds us that we are not the first to be called';[23] while Rolf Rendtorff, Professor of Theology at Heidelberg, concludes: 'The question confronting Christian theologians is whether they will continue to claim a shortened 'de-Judaised' Old Testament as Christian – then they should have the honesty and courage to declare this; if, however they would cite the Old Testament in its entirety – then they must concede its Jewish character and must refrain from challenging the right of the Jews to their own interpretation of the Bible.'[24]

Of course, the very term 'Old Testament' is not acceptable to Jews, and later (p. 66) we will speak of pejorative terminology. Although in certain circumstances (e.g. wine) 'Old' is preferable to 'New', the application to the Testaments implies replacement. Lacocque makes a point by referring to the Old Testament always as the 'Prime Testament'. Thoma, however, does not find the terminology offensive. The Old Testament is for Christians, he says, just as much a witness of the revelation of God as is the New. In order to gain an understanding of the Christian faith, the two must be taken as one. A Christian who was to relinquish or despise the Hebrew Scriptures would disclaim or abrogate his Christianity. It is therefore quite wrong, he asserts, to maintain that the very term 'Old Testament' is a Christian anti-Judaic interpretation of the Jewish Scriptures. From the very beginning, the disciples of Christ considered it a legacy by which the Christ-event was given a new relevance. The rabbinic scholars, from their point of view, also endeavoured to reactualise their biblical heritage. So though it could be said that 'Old' may have a negative connotation, Thoma holds that a mere change of terms would not add anything to Jewish–Christian understanding.

Before leaving the subject, mention should be made of the very special appeal of the Old Testament to African Christians.

They are attracted by its folk stories, its rituals, its emphasis on community, the tribal society it depicts, the stress on the Exodus theme of liberation, and sometimes even use it to excuse non-Christian customs such as sacrifice and polygamy. This has led on occasions to conflicts with missionaries who emphasise a Christianity based on the New Testament and European cultural tastes.[25]

The Pharisees

Moving forward into the New Testament period, we find the emergence of new understandings of the Pharisees – the fathers of rabbinic Judaism. Negative tones still linger, as can be seen by consulting the term in any dictionary, and even in the works of some scholars such as the German theologian Joachim Jeremias ('The Pharisees' devaluation of sin by casuistry and their idea of merit which makes sin innocuous had disastrous consequences'[26]), or Herbert Braun in his book *Jesus* ('The teachers of the law by their inconsistent behaviour failed to show love towards the people they taught'[27]) and many other sources, notably in French, German, Spanish and Italian. But the stereotype of the Pharisee and the identification of the term with 'hypocrite' has been challenged, not least by the work of pioneering Christian scholars such as Travers Herford and George Foot Moore and now by official Church declarations.

Paul Tillich explained that the Pharisees were the pious ones of their times and they represented the Law of God, the preparatory revelation without which the final revelation could not have occurred.[28] Eugene Fisher writes that modern scholarship has reclaimed the image of the Pharisees and depicted them as they really were. Quoting Talmudic condemnations of hypocrisy he shows that Jesus's condemnations of hypocrisy are typical Pharisaic teaching. 'To understand the teaching of Jesus', he writes, 'one must be open to the teaching of the Pharisees, for in many ways he showed himself to be one of them.'[29] The American theologian, Father John T. Pawlikowski, finds great identity between the ethics of Jesus and the ethics of the Pharisees which, he writes, were so advanced that they would find a resonance in contemporary theologies of liberation.[30]

These views of individual scholars have now received official endorsement in statements by the supreme Church bodies, Catholic and Protestant.

The Ecumenical Considerations on Jewish–Christian Dialogue issued by the World Council of Churches in 1983 states: 'Under the leadership of the Pharisees, the Jewish people began a spiritual revival of remarkable power which gave them the vitality capable of surviving the catastrophe of the loss of the Temple. As a Jew, Jesus was born into this tradition.' It also notes that some of the controversies reported between Jesus and the 'scribes and Pharisees find parallels within Pharisaism and are to be seen as internal Jewish controversies' (for full text see pp. 159ff.). The Vatican's 1985 'Notes on the Correct Way to Present the Jews and Judaism in Preaching and Catechesis in the Roman Catholic Church' also provides the much-maligned Pharisees with a long overdue rehabilitation, recalling that some of Jesus's doctrines are Pharisaic, that Paul considered his membership of the Pharisees as a title of honour, that the Pharisees warned Jesus of the risks he was running, that Pharisees are not mentioned in the account of the Passion, and that a negative picture of the Pharisees is inaccurate and unjust. If Jesus shows himself severe towards the Pharisees, this is because he was closer to them than to other contemporary Jewish groups (for the full text, see pp. 144ff.).

Jesus the Jew

The American writer, Norman Cousins, has commented that Jews and Christians have at least one thing in common: both have been unwilling publicly to live with the idea that Jesus was a Jew.[31] The American theologian, Roy Eckardt, has written that anti-Semitism is in part the war of Christians against Jesus the Jew.[32] I read this as that anti-Semitism is the triumph of the pagan in Christianity over the Judaic.

The Jewishness of Jesus, discovered over the past century by Christian and Jewish thinkers, has now become so accepted that

I even bought a lapel button in the US which stated succinctly: 'Jesus was raised in a kosher home.' It is staggering to realise how Jesus's Jewishness was ignored down the centuries and even in the new post-war climate the subject, until recently, was handled gingerly and obliquely in Church documents. The subject was taken up in Swiss Catholic[33] and Protestant[34] statements but seldom elsewhere. The progressive Rhineland Protestant synod stated; 'We confess to Jesus Christ the Jew, the Messiah of Israel and the Saviour of the World who connects the People of the World [i.e., the Gentiles] with the People of God [i.e., the Jews].'[35] It has been the individual theologians who have set the tone. Eugene Fisher tells of a Catholic bishop preaching in Chicago as early as 1931 who dared to suggest that Jesus was a Jew. He was greeted with hisses and boos and a woman called out: 'You're not a bishop. You're a rabbi.' 'Thank you madam', replied the bishop, 'that's just what they called Our Lord.'[36] Fisher adds that we need to correct traditional teaching that sought to approach Jesus in isolation from his people, for the denial of Jesus's Jewishness is a denial of his humanity.

Markus Barth in his book *Jesus the Jew* enumerates characteristics of Jesus which he discerns as typically Jewish:
— He respects the Jews as a Chosen People. He held on to his God, even in his hour of death, and to the Law, which he quoted to the end. He was a body and soul member of the Jewish community.
— He affirmed creation and did not denounce the earth as a vale of tears. God's election calls for decision and deeds.
— He eschewed cheap optimism. He knew the world was unredeemed. He did not preach original sin. He proclaimed forgiveness, healing, revival.

'We cannot believe in Jesus', writes Barth, 'without tending love and loyalty to the people out of which he came and whose mission among other peoples he confirmed for all times'.[37] Or as put by the US Catholic theologian Rosemary Ruether: 'Within the teaching of Jesus, I find no Christian anti-Jewishness. He neither regarded himself as messiah nor called for his followers to regard the law as superseded by a new covenant. He taught an ethical deepening of tradition as taught by the rabbis of his day. He stands within the prophetic tradition'.[38]

A growing number of Christian writers also now stress that Jesus's message was, after all, to the Jews. Thus Hans Küng, the controversial Catholic theologian, notes that in his time, Jesus could not have thought of a proclamation to the Gentiles. His message was very much a critique of the Judaism of his time – but the message was solely to his fellow Jews. Without Judaism there would be no Christianity and only with Judaism has Christianity a relationship of origin.[39] Mention should also be made of the writings of the British scholar, E. P. Sanders – the latest of which is *Jesus and Judaism* – which refutes theories by which Christian scholars have attempted to depict Jesus as opposing the Jewish religious authorities. For example, there was nothing unusual in his consorting with 'Sinners' since the Pharisees similarly laid great stress on repentance.[40] Allied to all this is the Jewishness of the Apostles who now emerge, it may be said, as the original 'Jews for Jesus' movement. The Vatican Council declaration recalls that the apostles and early disciples sprang from the Jewish people.[41]

In recent years, the Jewishness of Jesus has been expressly formulated and stressed in major Church declarations, including the World Council of Churches' 1982 document on relations with Jews and the Vatican's 1985 'Notes'. The latter devotes a section to the 'Jewish Roots of Christianity' starting with the words 'Jesus was and always remained a Jew. He was fully a man of his time and environment – Jewish Palestine of the first century' and it proceeds to list various indications of his Jewishness – from his circumcision and presentation in the Temple to his synagogue appearances and festival observances culminating in the Last Supper.[42] One sour note is that Arab Christians tend to read the statement that Jesus was a Jew as Jesus was an Israeli, and Arab Christian scholars and clerics often protest the new thinking on the Jewish origin and character of Jesus.

The death of Jesus

On the subject of the so-called 'Jewish guilt' for the crucifixion taught by the Churches down the ages and deeply ingrained in the Christian consciousness, *Nostra Aetate* marked a turning-point when it laid down: 'Not all that happened in Jesus' passion can be charged against all Jews then alive nor the Jews today. Jews should not be presented as accursed'.[43] The centuries of Jewish suffering caused by this accusation beggar the imagination and the retraction of the all-too-familiar teaching comes a thousand years too late to change the long record of Jewish martyrdom. Catholics have now rediscovered a remarkable statement from the sixteenth century Council of Trent which read:

> In the guilt of the crucifixion are involved *all* those who frequently fell into sin; for as *our* sins consigned Christ to death on the cross, most certainly those who wallow in sin and iniquity themselves crucify again the Son of God. This guilt seems more enormous in us than in the Jews since, according to the testimony of the apostle, if they had known it they would never have crucified the Lord of glory; while we, on the contrary, professing to know him yet denying him by our actions, seem in some sort to lay violent hands on him.

The same Council of Trent laid down that the crucifixion was Christ's free decision, and that all humanity theologically is responsible for the death of Jesus.[44] Tragically, these guidelines, laid down four centuries ago and so enlightened for their time, were consigned to oblivion and only recalled in the Vatican's 1985 'Notes'.

Official Protestant documents from Britain and Switzerland have also addressed themselves to the issue but elsewhere the problem has been largely ignored. The highly ambiguous statement issued by the Dutch Reformed Church in 1970 stated that 'the Jews rejected Jesus Christ, their messiah, out of zeal for the Law' and 'the Jewish people are alienated from God'.[45] These traditional concepts are so deeply ingrained in the Christian mentality that they cannot be expunged overnight and continue to be found in post-war thinking. Many of these were collected by the Catholic sister, Charlotte Klein, in her *Anti-Judaism in Christian Theology*.

She quotes many sources, mostly German, who continue to take the New Testament literally and uncritically. Thus Martin Dibelius in his *Jesus* writes: 'Out of Judaism grew the hostility that led to Jesus' death. In this sentence of death, Judaism passed judgement on itself'[46], and Leonhard Goppelt, author of *Jesus, Paul and Judaism* concluded: 'In the Jews' rejection of him, Jesus saw the conclusion of the conflict between God and Israel.'[47] The French Catholic father, Pierre Benoit, who lived and worked in Jerusalem, clearly and expressly attributes to the Jews the blame for the death of Jesus and holds them responsible for their subsequent fate. He continued to express such views even after the Vatican Council. 'On the plane of salvation history', he writes, 'the Jewish people *as such* committed a special fault. This may be compared with the original sin. Without involving the responsibility of each descendant, it makes him inherit the ancestral bankruptcy. Every Jew suffers from the ruin undergone by his people when it refused Christ at the decisive moment of its history.'[48]

Modern Biblical scholarship has growingly understood that anti-Jewish polemics were retrojected into the Passion story. Remarkably, as will be seen (pp. 91-2), the Vatican 1985 'Notes' recognise such a possibility. However, it is unrealistic to contemplate any revisions or modifications in the text of the Gospels. They will continue to be read and studied in their traditional form, with all its anti-Jewish nuances and influence, and even new translations or accompanying commentaries will not remove the sting. We will continue to hear of 'gospel truth'. A production in Jerusalem a few years ago of a Passion play made an honest effort to get away from anti-Jewishness but failed because this is inherent in the Gospels. Similarly attempts to revise the text of the Oberammergau Passion Play cannot eliminate the basic anti-Jewish image, and the annual recitation of Jewish perfidy in all churches at Easter-time remains one of the outstanding and seemingly insoluble obstacles in the Christian–Jewish relationship. Many Christian scholars are aware of this problem and are trying to take steps to solve it. In the words of Alan T. Davies:

> Christians need not choose between an ideological defense of their scriptures that wards off damaging criticism and the sad conclusion

that the New Testament is so wholly contaminated by anti-Jewish prejudice as to lose all moral authority. Instead, through careful study, Christians can isolate what genuine forms of anti-Judaism really colour the major writings and, by examining the historic genesis, neutralise their potential for harm.[49]

Continuity or discontinuity?

The theological core of the Jewish–Christian relationship is to be found in the Christian doctrine of discontinuity and supersessionism – the teaching of the election of Christianity and its assumption of God's covenant with mankind, previously entrusted to the Jews. The Jews lose their role as a chosen people and are superseded by Christianity. The key text is Romans 9-11 which has lent itself to diverse interpretations. Paul here expresses his sorrow for his Israelite brethren, because although theirs is the covenant, the Law, the promise and the origin of the Messiah, they have not accepted the Gospel. God has now brought forth the Church from among the Gentiles as well as the Jews. But God has not cast off Israel; salvation has come to the Gentiles to stir Israel to emulation. Henceforward Jews and Gentiles alike will be judged by their faith in Christ. However the Jews, as the recipients of the original covenant, retain a special role (they are the consecrated root of the olive tree in the famous metaphor in Romans 11); God's choice of them is irrevocable and His gracious gifts cannot be recalled. If they now prove disobedient, it is that ultimately they may receive mercy. Traditionally the elements in this passage stressing the disobedience of the Jews have been highlighted; it is only the new thinkers that have turned attention to accent the aspects of continuity.

However, even sympathetic interpreters find problems here. The Catholic thinker, Gregory Baum, has recounted his own frustrations. Initially he sought to show that anti-Jewish trends were later developments in Christian history, but had to change his mind in the realisation that passages in the New Testament reflect the conflict of Church and Synagogue in the first century.

All attempts of Christian theologians to derive a more positive conclusion from Paul's teaching in Romans 9-11 (and I have done this as much as others) are grounded in wishful thinking. As long as the Christian Church regards itself as the successor of Israel, as the new people of God, and proclaims Jesus as the one mediator without whom there is no salvation, no theological space is left for other religions and especially the Jewish religion. The central Christian affirmation on these lines negates the possibility of a living Judaism. According to this supposition, the religion of Israel has been superseded, the Torah abrogated, its promises filled in the Christian Church, the Jews struck with blindness, and whatever remains of the election to Israel rests as a burden upon them in the present age. If the Church wants to clear itself of the anti-Jewish trends built into its teaching a few marginal correctives (such as the Vatican 1965 Declaration) will not do. It must examine the very centre of its proclamation and reinterpret the meaning of the gospel for our times.[50]

The Protestant thinker, Roy Eckardt, analysing the text of Romans, concludes that Paul discerns great continuities between the Church and Israel, but that the effective discontinuity is greater. Christian attitudes, he finds, have been in three directions: 1. Israel has been cast off for all time; 2. Israel remains the elect people of God without essential qualification; 3. though Israel is not ultimately rejected of God, its place *in the present dispensation* is taken by the Church. Paul, says Eckardt, denies the first two statements and affirms the third. He concludes that if an ongoing solidarity of Christians with Jews is to be affirmed, it cannot be based on Romans 9-11. Still, to testify, as Paul does, that God has not finally rejected His people comprises a powerful rebuttal of the anti-Semitic Christian who asserts the opposite.[51]

But at the same time there are modern thinkers who stress Romans as a positive source for Jewish–Christian relations. The influential Protestant, Krister Stendahl, now Bishop of Stockholm and former Dean of the Harvard Divinity School, maintains that from a Christian perspective

we shall not come to the roots of anti-Semitism unless we learn from Paul that our witness has specific limits within God's mysterious and all-comprehensive plan. Paul's primary focus on Jews and Gentiles was lost in the history of interpretation and when it was retained the Church picked up the negative side of the mystery – Israel's 'No' to Jesus – but missed the warning against conceit and the feeling of superiority.[52]

Stendahl's remark that 'Paul did not preach about how I could be saved but about how gentiles could enter the Jewish covenant' has been confirmed in E. P. Sanders's landmark study *Paul and Palestinian Judaism*. The position of Paul is being increasingly seen as not placing the teaching of Jesus in opposition to Judaism but in showing how Christ fulfilled the Torah.[53] Kurt Hruby, alluding to the quotation in Romans that Israel neither stumbled nor fell, interprets Paul as saying that the aloofness of Israel will last through Christian history until all the Gentiles come in – and so Israel has a permanent function *vis-à-vis* the community of Christ and this means riches for the world. Israel then is not rejected or condemned but its existence is essential to Christianity on religious, and not merely humanitarian, grounds.[54] While Karl Barth, writing in 1942 and basing himself on Romans 9–11, concludes that Jews were the same elect people of God after the resurrection as before.[55]

This, then, is an introduction to the wider debate as to whether or not the Jews were rejected and Barth's view is now being heard in official Church statements. However, we must not think that the traditional theology is no longer with us. Writing in 1978 about the Protestant standpoint, Charlotte Klein finds that German theological books continue to start from such theses as: Judaism has been superseded and replaced by Christianity; it has scarcely any right to exist; and its teachings and ethical values are inferior to Christianity. To give some quotations:

> With the loss of the Temple, the last tie with the homeland was broken and the Jews as a people ceased to exist. Post-exilic Judaism is unhistorical and if it acts as a nation and intervenes in history, this merely shows its lack of trust in God. Obstinacy and guilt deprive the Jews of salvation. The Jews of today are different from those of the Old Testament. Not only did they not enter into the plane of fulfilment, but are in opposition to it (Leonhardt Goppelt).[56]

This line of thinking is significant in indicating the theological

rationale for Christian anti-Zionism to be found in certain Protestant circles and encountered in some World Council of Churches
contexts.

> Israel is obsolete and its existence meaningless. Its only eschatolo-
> gical hope is redemption by Christ. The tragedy of the Jews, indeed
> their guilt, lies in the fact that they do not regard themselves as
> precursors. Consequently, God's curse lies upon them. Israel can
> neither live nor die; only wait, blinded and hardened (written in
> 1959 by Michael Schmaus, author of the authoritative eight-
> volume *Katholische Dogmatik*).[57]

> Jews have forfeited all claims to be the Chosen People. Jesus' Jewish
> origin is merely of historical significance. Since his coming, the
> God whom the Jews worship is no longer the same as the God of
> the Christians. The Jews, in fact, are the synagogue of Satan and
> there is no possible way of Jew and Christian working together.
> The only possible relationship is the missionary one (J. G. Mehl).[58]

D. Judant, a French Catholic theologian of Jewish origin,
propounds a thoroughgoing replacement theology stressing the
guilt of the Jews. The whole Jewish community was involved in
the source of guilt, an act of spiritual treason. She notes two
disturbing facts: the suppression of the Jewish state in the year
70 and the continuing homelessness of the Jews (all this in a book
published in 1960).[59] And as a final quotation I mention the statement of Cardinal Bea, the person most responsible for the Vatican
Council's Declaration on the Jews: 'The destruction of Jerusalem
in the year 70 was an act of Divine judgement'.[60]

The fact is that the concept of discontinuity, while offensive
to Jews, is at least coherent for Christians. To admit a continuity
involves an element of mystery that requires considerable sophistication to accept. This is indeed to be found among the new
voices who reject the rejection. These include 'one-covenanters'
who see Jews and Christians as sharing the same covenant but
in different modes; and the 'two-covenanters' who find separate
but interrelated and complementary covenants for each. James
Parkes was a pioneer in challenging the idea that the Church is
the successor of the Synagogue, suggesting that Judaism is not
an alternative scheme of salvation but a different sort of religion.

He made the distinction that Judaism is directed to man as a social being while Christianity is directed to man as a personal being. Christianity seeks to transform man; Judaism to transform society. He objects to the 'Barthian metaphysics' which divides Jews and Christians into two dialectically related communities reflecting the 'yes and no of Divine mercy and judgement', and sees Christianity and Judaism as twin foci of a single revelation addressed to man in the individual and social dimensions of his life.[61] Krister Stendhal has made one of the pithiest comments: 'I am convinced that the only New Testament passage calling the Church 'Israel', namely Galatians 6:16, rests on a wrong reading of the text.'[62]

The leading Catholic theologians at the time of the Vatican Council adopted a 'mystery' approach in their explanations of the survival of Judaism, while remaining unequivocal in their affirmation of the centrality of Christ and the fulfilment brought by his coming to salvation history. They found ways to leave theological space after the coming of Christ but were content to attribute apparent contradictions to the element of 'mystery' in the divine plan of salvation.[63] By the 1970s, bolder initiatives can be discerned and these have been classified by Father John Pawlikowski into three models.[64]

1. There is a single covenant embracing both Jews and Christians; Christ was the point of entry for the Gentile world into the ongoing covenant established at Sinai. While Pawlikowski finds only one representative of this assertion – Monika Hellweg – it is relevant to quote Father Cornelius Rijk, who was at the forefront of the Catholic–Jewish dialogue. Although he would not have called himself a 'one-covenanter', his views appeared congruent when he wrote:

> Whatever we may think of the infidelity of the people of God [even he could not rid himself of this conviction], the Lord remains faithful. The distinction of two Gods – one of the Old Testament and one of the New Testament – is absolutely unacceptable. There is one God, one revelation, one salvation history. Not all the followers of Jesus fulfil the covenant nor has God turned away from those who did not follow Jesus in the newness.

He writes that the New Testament gives three different views on the relations between the Church and Judaism: the Church is a continuation of Judaism; the Church is a break with and opposed to Judaism; the Church is the fulfilment of Judaism. So, he says, both continuity and discontinuity are true. As long as the final kingdom of God has not been established on earth, God acts in an explicit way through Israel *and* the Church. The word of God is still addressed to Israel because, to quote Romans, the gifts and calls of God are irrevocable. God acts through the permanent value of the Hebrew Bible and the Jewish tradition as well as through the New Testament and the Christian tradition to establish His kingdom fully. God is faithful to His covenant and His people, and he quotes Cardinal Bea as saying: 'Through the Jews, the Old Testament remains a permanent message; otherwise, it might have become a dead letter.'[65]

2. Christianity and Judaism are distinctive religions with many complementary features and a shared biblical patrimony. Along these lines, Catholic thinkers have preferred to work with the idea of twin covenants, and he singles out Gregory Baum, Clemens Thoma and Franz Mussner.

Franz Mussner's *Tractate on the Jews* is an impressive and far-reaching document for a Catholic priest. His stated object is to prove that Judaism is a living reality which exists rightfully side by side with the Churches. Israel was not only the matrix of Christianity at its origin but remains at the root of the Church today. God's covenant with Israel was not abrogated by a later covenant. He stresses the special role of the Land of Israel in the religion of the Jews (a subject ignored by many and to which we will return in Chapter IV). Christians are not bound to a special country, but the land forms an integral part of Israel's election and covenant. In Judaism, religion, nationhood and land cannot be separated. He examines the Torah (which he is correctly careful not to translate as 'Law') and sees the joy in its observance. It is from Israel that knowledge of God has been brought to the Gentile world. Israel accompanies the Church throughout history until its end and the Church should finally acknowledge Israel as its companion on the road. The Jews have a role in the salvation of the world.

The Jew is the perpetual witness that history is not totally secular and Israel is a witness for the unfulfilment of complete Messianic salvation. He lists the inheritance that the Church has received from Judaism:

> Monotheism and Creation; the dignity of man as the image of God; faith not as an intellectual assent but as trust (*emunah*): the covenant theology, messianism, and the longing for a just world order and the duty of critique of injustice, political or social; the role of the Decalogue and the importance of conscience; the commemoration of the past in the liturgical present, which plays such a role in Passover and the Mass; and the belief in resurrection.[66]

3. Both Sinai and the Christ event represent Messianic experiences of which there can be an undetermined number. Pawlikowski associates this in particular with the writings of Rosemary Ruether, to whom we shall return. She feels the need to reformulate the traditional idea of the Christ Event as the final Messianic revelation and affirms that 'what Christianity has in Jesus is not the messiah but a Jew who hoped for the kingdom of God and died in that hope'.[67]

I would like here to refer to the so-called 'schism theology' which originated among radical Catholics. It was first posited in 1948 by a Belgian Benedictine, Dom Oehmen, who used the phrase 'schism in the Divine economy' with reference to the break between the Church and Israel. According to Oehmen, the schism has divided *Israel* into two parts: one believing, the other unbelieving. But in no sense are the Jews less elect today than they were prior to the birth of Christianity. Israel and the Church go side by side throughout history and no pejorative conclusions are to be drawn from the destruction of the Temple and the Diaspora.[68] Oehmen and the French theologian Paul Démann, who also propounded schism theology, arrived at their insights through the radical discovery of the message in Romans 9-11 that God had not disowned His people. Démann and Karl Thieme, a German Catholic, said that the coming of Jesus produced a tragic schism in God's people, damaging both communities. The Church is not the heir of the rightful Israel and what has happened is the thwarting of the Divine plan. The Jewish religion is incomplete without Jesus; Christianity is incomplete without the Jewish tradition. Thieme wrote that the schism between Church and Synagogue was not the first nor the last in salvation history; it was preceded by the schism between the northern and southern kingdom, followed by that between Eastern and Western Churches, Catholics and Protestants, etc. The schism between Church and Synagogue was of the same character and therefore the Jewish–Christian encounter has an ecumenical nature. The division is only temporary. However, for these theologians, the healing will come about by the conversion of the Jews, although not through human efforts. God alone can bring this about and the corollary is that missionary efforts are useless. The healing of the schism is not a phenomenon within the historical process but will only be achieved at the end of History.[69]

Heinrich Spaemann is another thinker who looks forward to the ecumenical fusion, organic as well as spiritual. In some manner, presumably by dialogue, Christians are required to promote the cause of that union with their Jewish *coreligionists* on the same basis that different branches of the Church seek visible union. The logical consummation would be for Jews to accept voluntary conversion.[70]

Naturally Jews are uncomfortable with these approaches even though they enable an existential coexistence. The presupposition of Christian triumph, even if eschatological, must leave the Jew in a position of tolerated inferiority. As long as some participating Christians envisage dialogue as a handle towards conversion, i.e. the Jewish acceptance of Jesus, even if only at the End of Days, the entire process as well as *all* those involved will inevitably be viewed with suspicion.

Critical views have been expressed in Christian circles. Thoma refuses to use the term 'schism' in the contemporary situation, saying that Christianity has not broken with Judaism in the same sense as applied to the schism between the churches of the East and West. The opposition between Judaism and Christianity is more profound, yet charged with more hope. He prefers to use the terms 'separation' or 'divorce'.[71] The American Protestant W. D. Davies finds a Christological factor expressed by Christianity which is non-negotiable even with its *mother-faith*, just as there is a centrality of Torah in Judaism which is non- negotiable. The dogmatic development of Christianity remains as the barrier to reducing the relations between the two faiths to a mere schism.[72] Some Protestant thinkers hold that the ancient covenant with Israel remains valid for the Jews; the new covenant by Jesus does not replace the ancient one but extends ancient promises to the Gentiles. The Jews have access to Divine Grace through fidelity to the original covenant. Parkes, Niebuhr and Tillich, for example, insist that the Jews do not need Christianity to be faithful to biblical promises.[73]

An original covenant doctrine has been propounded by J. Coert Rylaarsdam, the U.S. Reformed Church theologian.[74] He finds in the Bible two covenants, but they are both in the Old Testament. One of them is with Israel; one with David (he sees the covenant with Abraham as a retrojection). The Israel Covenant, expressed in the Hexateuch, has no eschatological intimations. The Land and the People are the signs of God's presence in the world. This covenant is absolute and primordial, past-oriented and decrees Divine determinism. Its theme of the people of God became part of the legacy of Israel. The David Covenant, which introduces the Messiah theme, is not a two-way covenant like the other, but a unilateral one. The chasm between man and God is bridged by the mystical figure of the Anointed, who is both human and Divine. This covenant is historical and contingent, it is future-oriented and decrees human freedom and responsibility.

In the Old Testament, the David Covenant was secondary. Christianity combined both covenants but reversed the priority, making the Israel Covenant subservient. The Christians who wrote the New Testament, which Rylaarsdam calls the most influential commentary ever written on the Old Testament, were a Jewish sect – sectarian because they took such a one-sided view of the relations between the two covenants. Judaism thought more historically than eschatologically (with the exception of some sectarians) but the New Testament is overwhelmingly eschatological and the writers of the New Testament thought they could fit the historical into the eschatological – and only later discovered that they were wrong. It has taken centuries to discover and rectify that mistake. The source of their recovery is knowledge of the foundation – the Hebrew Bible. So the same two covenants run through the Old Testament and the New Testament, which should therefore be divided horizontally, not vertically. His conclusion is that Judaism and Christianity revolve around the same two covenants, their relation is forever interdependent – and this is the basis for dialogue.

Official Church documents have been wrestling with these issues – and these statements after all, represent Church thinking; whatever the thoughts of individual theologians, it is the lead given by the Churches which in the end will be decisive. For the Catholics, *Nostra Aetate* was a landmark in its exploration of the Church's continuity with Israel, referring to 'the people of God', 'the stock of Abraham', 'election', 'promise' and 'covenantal revelation' in its references to Jews, language unprecedented in the Catholic Church. It gives the cue with the affirmation from Romans that God does not repent of the gifts He makes or the calls He issues.[75] The 1974 'Guidelines' and the 1985 'Notes' both affirm that the history of Judaism has continued to develop traditions rich in religious value and combat the belief that its mission ended with the advent of Jesus. Various national bishops' conferences have spoken out in like terms. The French bishops in 1973 declared that the precepts were received by the Christians without dispossessing the Jews who must be seen as a living religious reality[76] and the U.S. bishops affirmed that the Church can understand its own nature only in dialogue with Judaism.[77] This revolution in Catholic thinking is historic, although Gregory Baum warns that the theology of substitution is so deeply implanted that it operates also after it has been decided to adopt a more positive approach to the Jewish religion. Even Moltmann, who writes so sensitively about the Jews, finds no salvation apart from Jesus Christ and his teaching. In fact, says Baum, the structure of the Christian gospel is such that the theology of substitution emerges whenever Christians reflect on the dogmas of their faith.[78]

On the Protestant side, the theology is not so monolithic, which makes it possible for extreme liberalism and extreme conservatism to sit side by side. The Faith and Order Commission of the World Council of Churches in 1968 stated that the separation between the Church and the Jewish people has never been absolute. God formed the people of Israel and it was God's own will and decision that made this one distinct people with its special place in history. The Jewish people still maintain their significance for the Church. They make it manifest that God has not abandoned them.

> We reject the thought that their suffering down the ages is any proof of guilt. Why, in God's purpose, they have suffered in that way, we as outsiders do not know. What we do know, however, is the guilt of the Christians who have all too often stood on the side of the persecutors, instead of the persecuted. God will not abandon the Jewish people but will ultimately bring them salvation.

However, that understanding statement has a sting in its tail, as it continues: 'As long as the Jews do not worship with the Church the one God and the father of Christ, they are to us a perpetual reminder that God's promise is not yet realized in its fulness.'[79]

The most recent World Council of Churches document on Jewish–Christian dialogue, written with understanding and goodwill, gives practical guidelines for dialogue but carefully avoids taking a stand on the subject of discontinuity or election, although by implication it disparages the classical tradition which 'sees the Church replacing Israel as God's people' for its fateful consequences, leading to distorted views and unjustified actions.[80]

Various national churches have tried to make contributions to clarify the issues. The Council of the Evangelical Church in Germany declared in 1975: 'The New Testament transferred basic elements of Old Testament covenantal thinking to the Christian community. Jews and Christians both understand themselves as people of God. Despite their division, *both* are called and ordained to be witnesses of God in this world and to move forward toward the future fulfilment of His reign.'[81] The Swiss Protestants in 1977 issued the following statement: 'As God has not rejected His people, the Church cannot call itself the new people of God or the new Israel. The Church cannot take over the covenant from the Jewish people. Israel and the Church coexist, united in many ways but divided on basic points.' It lists the dividing points as: 'the Jewish attitude to Jesus; the blame attached by many Christians to Jews for the crucifixion; for the stress on justice rather than grace; for insistence on ritual law; and because some Christians have seen Jews as accursed to the extent of extermination. The two have also been divided by Church attitudes on the Holocaust and the State of Israel.' The uniting points include: the Jewishness of Jesus and of his teachings; the Old Testament basis of the New Testament; the fact that the Church issued out of Judaism; that the first Christians were Jews, and that Christianity has taken many practices from Judaism.[82] A final example is the highly refreshing document prepared in 1977 by the British Working Group for the World Council of Churches' Consultation on the Church and the Jewish People. Although not enjoying official endorsement, it is a notable Protestant statement of a non-supersessionist theology based on a profound understanding of Jewish self-definition and a recognition of the post-war resurgence of the Jewish people centred on the State of Israel, seen as the highest spiritual purpose of the Jews. The people of the two covenants, it says, together constitute the continuing people of God who should enrich and encourage one another.[83]

The Swiss document just quoted mentions the apposition between justice and grace. Conservative Christians continue to condemn the Law and its observance. They translate 'Torah' as 'Law' giving it negative implications, lacking the understanding of Law as a spiritual confrontation with God the Lawgiver. Thus Père Benoit can still write that it is the fault of the Jews that in its historic realisation, the system of Law failed and that God's help and grace are no longer given to the Jew.[84] We still encounter time and again this line of thinking familiar since the early centuries since Christ. Only gradually are some Christian theologians reaching the conclusion that Law presupposes God's gift of grace to man and is itself grace. One of these is Rosemary Ruether, who points out that the original criticism of Jesus against legalistic aspects was an internal Jewish criticism, Jew against Jew. So if applied today, criticism of legalism and hypocrisy should be applied internally to one's own people and to *Church* leaders, and not directed to another people with which the Church no longer identifies. The modern equivalent of Pharisees, she suggests, is theologians. She goes on to write that the most difficult schism to criticise is alleged Jewish particularism against so-called Christian universalism. What was seen once as the universal mission of the Church is on the wane and today survives mainly in Western imperialism and neo-colonialism. Christianity itself has only conquered completely within the area that is heir to the Greco-Roman tradition; so from a world perspective, Christianity is highly particularistic, one particularism among many other particularisms. On the other hand, universalism and particularism are two sides of the relationship between Judaism and other people with what is generally expressed through the concept of the Noachian laws.[85]

Mission to the Jews

One of the most divisive issues on the Jewish–Christian agenda is that of mission to the Jews. The traditional Christian attitude has been that the Jew was allowed to continue to exist – as an essential object of mission. His non-Christianisation delayed the Second Coming and therefore mission to the Jews was integral to the Christian worldview. Old-type mission is now confined to certain Churches and theologians but no longer among Catholics, and seldom in the Protestant mainstream. Even those who insist on the continuation of mission tend to be more sophisticated than their predecessors. They are aware of Jewish hypersensitivities on this subject and of the blot of Christian mission in the record of anti-Semitism but they reject any suggestion that one religion is as good as another or that God is not redemptively active in world history. They feel that the Christian fulfilment in Jesus Christ must be proclaimed, and especially to the Jew, as the recipient of revelation. Thus Jakob Jocz, lecturing at Princeton Seminary, can state that the Church in confrontation with the Synagogue can be the Church only if she is wholeheartedly a missionary Church, for only in confrontation with the Synagogue does the centrality of Jesus Christ for the Christian faith become truly visible. The moment we profess Christ as our Lord, he asserts, a missionary situation is created and Jews cannot be exempted from that mission. If Christianity has no Gospel for the Jews, it has no Gospel for the world.[86]

But there are new winds and the remarkable change in the Catholic church will be described in chapter 3 (see pp. 84-5). In the Protestant world, Reinhold Niebuhr, who is seminal to contemporary liberal thinking on the Jews, wrote that mission was wrong because the two faiths, despite their differences, are sufficiently alike for the Jew to find God more easily in terms of his own religious heritage than by subjecting himself to the hazards of guilt feeling involved in a conversion to a faith which, whatever its excellences, must appear to him as the symbol of an oppressive majority culture.[87] This has been taken up by thinkers who have characterised mission to the Jews as a denial of God's covenant with Israel. Only by total renunciation of such mission is the way open to true dialogue. Recognising the continuing role of the Jewish people in the divine economy, theologians are increasingly challenging the concept of Christian mission.

The American Lutheran, Harold H. Ditmanson, has distinguished three main contemporary attitudes towards mission to the Jews. The first asserts that the Church has a mission to all men, including the Jews. The scope of mission cannot be restricted but the Jews are not to be made the *special* targets of Christian mission. If they come within the reach of the normal evangelistic witness of a Christian congregation they are not to be excluded. This is the established policy of most mainline Churches. The second attitude holds that while the Church has a mission to all men, it has a special mission to the Jews. Because of the special relationship between Judaism and Christianity, the Jews should be turned to the Messiah Jesus and once again become a light to the nations. This represents the thinking of conservative Christians who are convinced that without an explicit faith in Christ, a person must be condemned to everlasting punishment. The third attitude asserts that the Church has a mission to all men – except the Jews, a view growing out of deep sensitivity to the unique relationship between Judaism and Christianity. This theology of mutual recognition and coexistence sees the Church and the Jewish People as together forming the one People of God. Witness is not excluded but in relation to the Jews is seen as an ecumenical engagement – a true dialogue – for the sake of fuller understanding and a mutual ministry of justice rather than for conversion.[88] This last attitude has been graphically expressed by Roy Eckardt:

> The Jewish people are already with God, participants in an age-old covenant. They do not have to be 'saved'. The Christian is the man who dares to hope that he belongs in some all-decisive way to the family of Jews. If the Jewish people are not already among the family of God, we who are gentiles remain lost and without hope. By seeking to do away with the Jewish community, the missionary attitude is an assault on the very foundation of Christianity.[89]

Official Protestant statements since the war have often, from the Jewish vantage, been far from satisfactory. Many of these continue to be rooted in past prejudices and sometimes betray little awareness of post-Holocaust sensitivities. Of course the pluralistic composition of Protestantism must be remembered, with the impossibility of an *ex cathedra* statement at the top and with the input of variegated churches, including the less liberal, requiring integration. Forthright statements by Protestant theologians do not easily rise to the uppermost levels.

The document of the First Assembly of the World Council of Churches in 1948 was ambivalent, the result of conflicting statements prepared by two subcommittees which were both incorporated without any attempt at reconciliation. On the one hand it says: 'To the Jews, our God has bound us in a special solidarity, linking us together in His design', a text seized on by those seeking to pursue dialogue. But the document also says: 'Jesus Christ said "Go ye into the world and preach the Gospel to every creature." The fulfillment of this commission requires that we include the Jewish people in our evangelistic task. The Church has received its spiritual heritage from Israel and is in honour bound to render it back in the light of the Cross. We have therefore to proclaim to the Jews "The Messiah for whom you wait has come."' As mentioned, it regrets the neglect of the mission to the Jews and states that parishes and churches should have special ministers for this task.[90]

The World Council of Churches' 1968 Faith and Order Commission statement also spoke in two voices, although in some ways it was an improvement on the earlier pronouncement. 'If we stress the Church as the body of Jesus Christ', it says,

> the Jews are outside and the Church's mission is to bring them to acceptance of Christ. The Church and the Jewish people can be thought of as forming the one people of God and the attitude to Jews should be different from that to other non-believers. We reject proselytising in the sense of corruption of witness, in cajolery, undue pressure, or intimidation or improper words.'[91]

Most recently, the 1983 WCC document on the Jewish–Christian dialogue tries to steer a tricky course through the gamut of attitudes represented in various constituent churches. It refers to the broad spectrum of approaches and concludes: 'Dialogue can be described by mutual witness but only when the intention is to hear the others in order better to understand their faith, hopes, insights and concerns. The spirit of dialogue is to be fully present to one another in full openness and human vulnerability.'[92] It is a vague conclusion – a compromise between the tendencies of a majority of the formulating group and the requirements of WCC elements who retain a strong missionising objective.

Individual churches have drawn less ambiguous conclusions. The first to speak out was the Dutch Reformed Church which stated that the Church should abandon its attempt to convert the Jews 'but rather as befitting the younger sister try to enter into dialogue with an elder brother'.[93] Instead of mission it called for Christian–Jewish solidarity and a relationship of trust and respect for the other's identity. The 1980 Synod of Protestant Churches of the Rhineland made the striking statement: 'We believe that Jews and Christians in their calling are witnesses of God in front of the world and in front of each other. Therefore we are convinced that the Church has the testimony to bring its mission to other people – but not to the Jewish people.'[94] This stirred strong opposition in certain German circles where theologians often stand squarely behind mission. A counter-document produced by a group of well-known theologians at the University of Bonn stressed that the Church cannot give up teaching the Gospel to *all* people.[95] This may be cited as another example where the Christian–Jewish encounter in the modern world has proven highly divisive, within both faith-communities.

The World Lutheran Federation comprises churches with a broad spectrum of views on the subject, including many deeply committed to mission. The latter advocate dialogue but within carefully circumscribed limits. The 1975 Council of Evangelical Churches in Germany said that both Christians and Jews must give witness to their own faith. 'Missionary practices exist even today which give Jews justified cause for suspicion. Such practices are decidedly rejected by the Church. However, such misuse does not release Christians from an authentic endeavour to render account according to the Gospels. Faith must not remain silent.' It added that mission and dialogue are two dimensions of one Christian mission, although realising that this sounds ominous to Jews. Christians, it concludes, need to talk to Jews for the sake of the Christians.[96] The Lutheran World Federation in 1975 stated:

> It is a misconception that Jews be isolated in a class by themselves and then singled out for exclusive missionary attention or excluded from Christian mission altogether. That would be to assure that we are the haves, the others the have-nots. Christians, no less than others, are sinners. . . In witnessing to Jews, we must be aware of the unique relationship, both in continuity and discontinuity'.[97]

In 1983 a Jewish-Lutheran dialogue met in Stockholm on the occasion of the Luther Year, and the Lutherans issued a document rejecting Luther's notorious anti-Jewish teachings and a joint statement repudiated 'any organised proselytising'.[98] These documents were adopted by the Lutheran World Assembly in the following year and recommended to the constituent churches.

The Evangelicals

Mission is, of course, a top priority for the evangelical churches, whose theological sights are set on the Second Coming. To bring this nearer, they feel it their mission to bring the rest of mankind to a belief in Jesus. Estimates speak of 60,000-80,000 evangelical missionaries in various parts of the world, including North America.

The Evangelicals are distinguished by a number of theological considerations. One is the centrality of the Bible; everything is viewed through the lens of Scripture, the word of God. Their stress on the infallibility of the literal Bible text is parallel to the belief of Orthodox Jews, and indeed the debate over 'inerrancy' has a familiar ring to Jewish ears. Other emphases are on the person of Jesus and on the 'born again' experience. In the past such Christians were often called 'fundamentalists', meaning that they had returned to the fundamentals of the Church, but today this term is generally reserved for the highly conservative, right-wing, anti-intellectual Evangelists.

The number of evangelical sub-groups is legion. A scholar I met in the US was proud of his achievement in reducing them to a mere twenty-three *categories*. The main core is in the United States where the Evangelicals claim between thirty and sixty million adherents. One cannot generalise about their attitudes to Jews and Judaism as they consist of such disparate groups. The overall attitude to ecumenism is negative; they prefer to use the term 'fellowship' but on examination this tends to be limited to co-operation with other evangelical groups.

Jews are basic to their *Weltanschauung*, especially as the return of the Jews to their promised land is an essential element in the course of events leading to the Second Coming. Major segments look on Jews everywhere as the chosen people. The more liberal and sophisticated say that this chosenness is an accepted fact and it must remain a mystery how they will eventually accept Jesus. They will enjoy a national salvation in God's own way in the Messianic age, but meanwhile they should be left to fulfil their own destiny. Jerry Falwell, leader of the 'Moral Majority', has said:

'God has blessed America because we have blessed the Jews. God has raised up America in these last days for the cause of world evangelisation *and* for the protection of His people, the Jews. I don't think America has any other right or reason for existence other than these two purposes.'[99] Many evangelicals deeply believe that America has been divinely blessed for its favourable treatment of the Jews and Israel.

Inevitably in such a diverse aggregation, anti-Semitic views are not absent. I do not know who coined the sick neo-Nazi bumper sticker 'Gas a Jew for Jesus' reported to have appeared on the West coast of the US but evangelical endorsements have appeared for the notorious anti-Semitic libel 'Protocols of the Elders of Zion'. A more simple reaction is that if the Jews do not accept Jesus, 'how can we even talk to them'. A few years ago, Reverend Bailey Smith, then President of the large and influential Southern Baptists Conference, stated that God does not hear the prayers of Jews. This caused considerable consternation in the Jewish community but on investigation it proved to be not an expression of anti-Semitism but of a theological position which would apply to all who do not accept Christ.[100] Nevertheless, a sampling of Evangelical broadcasts in America's 'Bible Belt' around Easter-time still reveals the constant reiteration of the 'Jesus killed by the Jews' theme. Officially, however, many Evangelicals have taken strong stands against anti-Semitism. In 1972, the Southern Baptists passed a resolution to fight anti-Semitism as 'Jews, along with all other persons, are equally beloved of God'. The major mouthpiece 'Christianity Today' has constantly condemned all forms of anti-Semitism while admitting that manifestations do exist among Evangelicals. Some of these groups distinguish between Jews in Israel and those in the Diaspora; the former are God's instruments but the latter are accorded no special status and are lumped together with all other non-believers.

Some have maintained a high-power missionary outreach to Jews but many have lowered their missionary profile to Jews, distinguishing between proselytising and witnessing. The centrist attitude, represented by 'Christianity Today', holds that while

Jews must expect evangelists to seek adherents to the Christian faith, there is a commitment to religious freedom. This also means that every religious group has the right to practice and propagate its own faith – and to allow other groups the right to seek converts, providing no unworthy pressures are employed.

The attitudes of the Evangelicals pose a dilemma for Jews, especially in the United States. For one thing, they feel uncomfortable in their encounter with people who basically call into question the authenticity of Judaism. For another, they are concerned with the appeal to some young Jews, such as those who have established the 'Jews for Jesus' movement. Especially, the Jews, who have by and large maintained Liberal views, find it difficult to co-operate with these elements with their reactionary agenda, opposing feminism, abortion, gay rights, etc., and favouring school prayers which to Jews threaten the basic separation of Church and State. The dilemma is to weigh these issues against the cause of Israel where the Evangelicals, out of their own theological motivations, can provide a loud pro-Israel voice which at certain junctures – such as during the 1982 Lebanon War – was seen as vital to Israel's information efforts in the United States. Some Jewish spokesmen have stated categorically that Jewish and Evangelical interests are diametrically opposed and have expressed alarm at preaching for enactments of 'Christian values in society'. Others note that the Evangelicals have not sought breaches of democratic procedure and concluded that their followers are not captive on political and economic issues to the preachers. Paradoxically, extreme Orthodox groups, such as the Rabbinical Alliance, have proved the most supportive of the Evangelicals in view of an identity of interests: they too oppose abortion, permissiveness, feminism, gay rights, favour school prayer and support Israel.

Anti-Semitism and the Holocaust

A number of Christian scholars have by now examined the chain, extensively acknowledged, leading from Christian anti-Semitism to Auschwitz. One historian has listed in parallel columns Nazi law and Canon anti-Jewish law, while the notorious Julius Streicher at his Nuremberg trial stated in his defence 'I was only repeating what Luther said'.[101]

Already in October 1945, shortly after Germany's defeat, the surviving leaders of the German Protestant Churches issued the Stuttgart Declaration of Guilt for the suffering inflicted by the Germans during the Nazi era – but said nothing explicitly about the fate of the Jews. It took five more years before they issued a statement admitting: 'Through omission and silence before the God of Mercy, we were co-responsible for the wickedness which was committed against Jews by members of our own people.' But even then the motives for the statement were humanitarian rather than a call for rethinking of Christian theological attitudes.[102] By now Christians of all denominations have condemned anti-Semitism – 'a sin against God' as the World Council of Churches put it in 1948 – although some of the statements are tepid, reminding one of Roy Eckardt's comment on the Vatican Council Declaration on the Jews: 'It would have redeemed a little – in the 13th century.'[103]

A powerful analysis of Christian anti-Semitism has come from Rosemary Ruether, for whom anti-Semitism is the left hand of Christology and who asks: 'Is it possible to say "Jesus is Messiah" without implicitly saying at the same time "The Jews be damned"'? [104] The fundamental roots of Christian anti-Judaism, she says, lie not in Gentile anti-Semitism but in the intra-Jewish religious sectarianism. The basic antagonism is one of a sectarian claim by the Church to represent the true heir of the election of Israel over and against normative Judaism. The heart of the conflict lies in the claim of Christians to be the true Israel, and this sets Christian anti-Judaism fundamentally apart from pagan anti-Semitism.

The Church said the Jews read the letter of the Scriptures but not the spirit and were blind to the promises of grace. This was developed until the Jews were seen as demonic. The anti-Judaic myth was strong in the Church Fathers who developed two dominant themes: the election of the Gentiles and the repro-bation of the Jews (connected with their responsibility for the death of Jesus Christ) and the inferiority of Jewish law, cult and understanding of Scriptures. By now Christian pseudo-universalism had become Christian particularism with only one path to God.

Modern radical anti-Semitism is not a *direct* continuation of Christian anti-Semitism but Christianity provided the essential background for this development. Without twenty centuries of Christian vilification of the Jews, it is impossible to understand why it was the Jews, rather than some other group, who became the main Nazi victims. Christian anti-Judaism was not genocidal in the modern sense; in Christian terms, the 'final solution' of the Jewish problem was conversion.

The Church, which fomented a cultural myth about the Jew as Christ-killer, must now meet itself as Jew-killer. Those who pursued the Jews for deicide are now guilty of at least laying the ground for genocide. In the long run, Ruether is deeply pessimistic. She suspects that anti-Judaism is too deeply embedded in the foundations of Christianity to be rooted out without destroying the whole structure. We may have to settle, she writes, for ecumenical goodwill that lives with theological inconsistency and opts for a pragmatic *modus operandi*.[105]

In the view of Friedrich Heer of Vienna University, anti-Semitism is a historical manifestation of a much deeper cancer in Christianity. It is part of a general disregard of humankind and the world, due to the dominance in Christian theology of the Augustinian principle which views the world *sub ratione peccati* – the theology of the curse leading to fatalism and despair. 'We must replace the Augustinian principle with a return to the Hebrew Bible's roots of Christ's own piety and to the original faith in which humanity felt itself to be both God's creature and God's responsible partner', he asserts.[106] In England a courageous stand has been taken by the Bishop of Salisbury, Chairman of the Church of England Doctrine Commission, who has called on the Churches to disown the 'distorted features' of the New Testament if they are to have clean consciences concerning race relations. Christianity, more than any other religion, he has written, has succumbed to the disease of racism and the primary reason for this was 'the poison of anti-Judaism, developed into anti-Semitism, which Christianity has spewed out from the earliest times.'[107]

Facing the Holocaust directly, Father Gregory Baum asks:

> What if God is addressing the Church anew through the awful message of the Holocaust? The Holocaust teaches the Church that any monopolistic Divine truth or any form of ecclesiastical self-elevation will eventually translate itself into social attitudes and political action and generate grave injustices that eventually accumulate to become major crimes'.[108]

In Europe some Christian thinkers have reached extreme conclusions. Thus Johann-Baptist Metz of Munster feels that Christian theology is now dependent on its own victim, the Jews of Auschwitz, for any hope of understanding itself,[109] while Jürgen Moltmann finds the suffering Jesus of the Cross in the person of an innocent child hanged in the notorious death camp: 'Only the Jew imprisoned alone with his God in the abyss has the right to answer the question "Where is God?" Not we Christians out of Auschwitz who sent the Jew into such a situation of despair or at least left him to it.'[110] The American Protestant, Franklin Littell, has described the Holocaust as 'the major event in recent Church history', signalising as it does the rebellion of the baptised against the Lord of History. 'Christianity has been put to the test by the apostasy of millions of the baptised by being willing or silent accomplices in the murder of most of the European Jews.'[111]

These are outspoken voices, not necessarily characteristic. Various writers feel that despite efforts on the part of ecclesiastical authorities and some theologians, not much in the Churches' attitude has really changed. There have been suggestions that awareness of the Holocaust recedes with the passing of the years. This has been discerned in some circles in the World Council of Churches, especially after the Orthodox churches, with their lack of awareness of the subject, were integrated in 1961 and the rise to a dominating role in the 1970s of churches in the Third World with their own agenda, which at best see the Holocaust as just one in a long series of world atrocities, with no unique dimension and certainly one for which the Third World cannot be held responsible. Charlotte Klein concludes that Christian post-war theology speaks of Judaism as it did before the war, certainly in the European ambience in which she specialised.[112] With the Vatican the basic dilemma remains the assumption of an innate triumphalism which, even if only eschatological, continues to promote a psychology of superiority which can undermine dialogue with all non-Christian faiths, including Judaism notwithstanding the recognition of a special relationship. With all churches, the problem has to be faced that even when they condemn anti-Semitism they are continuing to propound the same views that have contributed to anti-Semitism in the past, notably teaching, or at least implying, that Jews were responsible for the death of Jesus (and even if limited to 'some contemporary Jews' the impact is pejorative), that salvation is only attainable through Christianity, and that Judaism is anachronistic, condemned by its excessive legalism and particularism. In the words of the disciple and student of James Parkes, Robert Everett:

> Condemnation of anti-Semitism by churches is only half of the real battle. Christianity must fight if anti-Semitism is to be truly condemned and eliminated. The other half of the battle consists of Christian theology actually confronting and eliminating those anti-Jewish teachings which have been responsible for theologically justifying Christian anti-Semitism for nearly two thousand years. Failure to fight the battle completely will leave the Church in the paradox of condemning something that it theologically justifies.

He feels that this tradition is so ingrained that changing it will require more than pointing to the Holocaust.

> If this tradition is to be eliminated from Christian theology, the theologians will need to prove that Christian knowledge and self-definition is not dependent on this tradition nor threatened by its elimination – with the realisation that the only real results the Christians will have in changing the tradition will be by proving that Christian theology does not need to justify Jewish suffering or hatred of the Jewish people in order to be Christian.[113]

Parkes himself proposed four changes in Christian theology: (a) Recognition that the New Testament is incorrect in its teachings about Jesus; (b) the Church needs to qualify its claims to religious truths; (c) it should shift its emphasis from the Christocentric to the theocentric; (d) it should relate to Judaism on the basis of a theology of equality.[114]

New insights

To end this chapter, I will bring a few of the more striking statements on Christian–Jewish relations today in a world of dialogue, which is a somewhat misleading term, as it means talking to one another, whereas the emphasis should be on listening to each other. At the same time, we will never forget that alongside our shared heritage, we are distinct religions and our objective is not syncretism.

Allan Brockway, Secretary of the World Council of Churches' Consultation of the Church and the Jewish People, has recently suggested that the WCC 1983 document on relations with the Jewish People develops the *theory* of dialogue as far as possible for the present (even if practice lags far behind). He proposed that the next stage should be one of 'regrouping' in which both sides on their own should look inward and assess what has been learned in the post-war dialogue. Jews, for example, should reflect seriously, he says, on what it means for them to live in a world in which the Church is on their side rather than opposing and persecuting them. To Jews who question this assumption, he points to renunciation of the deicide charge, opposition to anti-Semitism and the affirmation of God's covenant with Israel. To Christians, he calls for a reconsideration of the Messiahship of Jesus, the incarnation and the resurrection in the light of the continuing Jewish denial and of the contemporary scientific world view.[115]

There has been argument as to whether one can speak of a 'Judeo-Christian' tradition and in the next chapter we will examine Jewish views (p. 64-5). For Paul Tillich this was an historical and present reality, not a pious fiction manufactured to promote goodwill between adherents of both faiths. Jews and Christians, he maintained, are united in so far as both regard a unique series of events recorded in the Hebrew Bible as revelatory. They belong to each other in a special way: it may be said that Christianity is a Jewish heresy and that Judaism is a Christian heresy. Christianity will always need the corrective influence of Judaism. Judaism is a permanent ethical corrective of sacramental Christianity.[116] Ruether finds the phrase 'Judeo-Christian' a misleading oversimplification. She calls on Judaism to re-examine its misunderstandings of Christianity: that it is polytheistic (as it sees the Trinity); that good works have no place in Christianity; that it espouses blind faith; that it is ascetic and other-worldly (in contrast to Jewish this-worldliness); that it is pessimistic; that it maintains belief in magic and superstition; that it believes only Christians can be saved. These, she finds, are Jewish misnomers.[117]

According to John Pawlikowski, Christianity would be enriched from aspects of Jewish tradition, especially its affirmation of life, its sense of peoplehood and community, its positive valuation of sexuality, its close interweaving of prayer and social action, its sense of creation as a visible experience and locale of God's presence, its emphasis on dynamism over form in religious experiences.[118] Ruether goes further. To accept Jewish covenantal existence, Christians must learn the story of the Jews after Jesus; they must accept the Oral Torah as an authentic alternative route by which the biblical past was appropriate and carried on. This requires the learning of a suppressed history. For Christians to incorporate the Jewish tradition after Jesus into their theological and historical education would ultimately involve the dismantling of the Christian concept of history and the demythologising of the myth of the Christian era. The suppression of Jewish history and experience from Christian consciousness is tacitly genocidal. What it says, in effect, is that the Jews have no further right to exist after Jesus.[119]

Another positive statement comes from Markus Barth:

> The intervention by Jews on behalf of social justice, their generosity, their joy in work, their steadfastness in suffering shame us. Often they carry out what was entrusted to the Church. Their survival and security, in Israel or in the Diaspora, is essential for the continuing existence and faith of the Church if the Church is not to become a pagan culture and social institution but is to

represent, together with the Jews, the one people of God on earth.[120]

And Krister Stendahl goes a step further, saying:

> Christian theology needs a new departure, we cannot find it on our own but only with the help of our Jewish colleagues. We must plead with them to help us. We must ask if they are willing, in spite of it all, to let us again become part of their family – relatives who believe themselves to be a peculiar kind of Jews. Something went wrong at the beginning. Is it not possible for us to recognise that we parted ways not according to but against the will of God?[121]

And on to Paul Van Buren in *Discerning the Way*, the first of his four-volume work on 'The Jewish-Christian reality'. He writes:

> We define ourselves as gentiles by reference to the Jews because Our Way has no starting point and no possible projection except by reference to the Way in which Jews were walking before we started and are walking still. The first walkers who produced the Apostolic Writings were convinced that our Way could only be walked with the help provided by carrying us with the Book that Jesus and all his apostles had understood to be their own and only Scriptures – which St Jerome liked to call 'the Hebrew truth'. That book, backed as it was by the continuing vitality of the Jewish people, most of whom at least hear it in its original tongue, reminds us that we are gentiles, not Jews, although gentiles who worship Israel's God. In everything that has to do with our future movement along the Way, we are profoundly dependent on the Jews. We use a Jewish vocabulary (such as "law", "prophets", "creation", "covenant", "sin", "repentance", "holiness", "Sabbath", "judgement", "reassurance"). The Church developed the view that the Jews have been cast off and developed the teaching of contempt. The Holocaust and the founding of the State of Israel have forced a re-thinking. If God was not faithful to His people, why should we assume He will be any more faithful to the gentile Church? What is our final hope in the Jewish–Christian conversation? To be one? How? Not one assimilating the other. Maybe walking side by side.[122]

And for a Catholic voice, let us return to Cornelius Rijk:

> One critique of Vatican II was that it spoke about Jews in Christian categories and showed no understanding for how Jews think about

or see themselves. Later documents show development in this area, with their emphasis on reciprocity and their exclusion of proselytism. They emphasise the permanence of the religious values in Judaism and advocate social collaboration between the two religions because both have the same concept of human dignity. Common involvement in the service of the world in the name of justice, covenant and charity is an efficacious way of understanding each other, even on the theological level. Moreover, Jewish–Christian relations are essential for Christian unity as this unity cannot be attained without returning to the sources of Christianity.[123]

And finally, the future vision of Roy Eckardt:

The Christian community will venerate the Hebrew Bible on its own terms. That community will do its utmost to restore a non-exclusionary Jesus to the circle of his followers. That community will have been delivered from pagan-Gentile distortions and returned to a life-giving Jewishness. That community will represent and implement the moral and spiritual universalism for which the synagogue stands. That community will have abandoned its fatal proclivity to absolutise things that are relative. That community will be victorious over a missionising policy and attitude that betrays Jewish integrity and truth. That community will have redeemed itself from the anti-Israelism that is a cover for anti-Semitism. That community will fully recognise and proclaim to the world the massive Jewish contribution to our conceptions and applications of social justice, to the modern welfare state, to international cooperation, to human freedom, to the solidarity and pricelessness of the family, to education, and to new ways of thought and life for Christendom and within modern nationhood. Above all, that community will offer continuing thanksgiving for the ongoing presence of God's people, Israel.[124]

I have chosen to end this chapter with a mosaic of views reflecting the most progressive Christian voices in the dialogue. They are way ahead of the pack and our hope is that they are the pacesetters. As we have seen there remain grey and even black areas, but our fifty-year perspective has also shown us advances that in many respects can be defined as no less than revolutionary.

Notes

1 J. Parkes, *The Conflict of the Church and the Synagogue*, New York, 1961, p. 376.
2 *Christian–Jewish Relations* Vol. 19 No. 1 (March 1986), p. 48.
3 J. Parkes in *Anti-Semitism and the Foundations of Christianity*, ed. A. Davies, New York, 1979, p. viii.
4 R. Stone in *Christian–Jewish Relations*, Vol. 15 No. 3 (September 1982), pp. 37ff.
5 J. Maritain, *Redeeming the Time*, London, 1943, pp. 133ff.
6 E. Fleischner, *Judaism in German Christian Theology*, Metuchen, N.J., 1975, p. 24.
7 A. T. Davies (ed.), *Anti-Semitism and the Christian Mind*, New York, 1969, p. 110
8 I. Goldstein, *Jewish Perspectives*, Jerusalem, 1985, pp. 394ff.
9 H. Croner (ed.). *More Stepping-Stones to Jewish-Christian Relations*, New York, 1985, pp. 32-3.
10 H. Croner (ed.), *Stepping-Stones to Jewish-Christian Relations*, New York, 1977, pp. 69-72.
11 R. Stone *op.cit.* (note 4), p. 40.
12 C. Thoma, *A Christian Theology of Judaism*, New York, 1980, p. 26.
13 M. Noth, *The History of Israel,* New York, 1958, pp. 447ff.
14 A. Lacocque in *Biblical Studies*, ed. L. Boadt, H. Croner and L. Klenicki, New York, 1980, p. 120.
15 *Stepping-Stones* (see note 9), p. 1.
16 *Ibid.*, p. 62.
17 *Ibid.*, pp. 73ff.
18 Documents published by World Council of Churches, Programme Unit in Faith and Witness, March 1974.
19 In an unpublished paper, 'The Theology of Judaism'.
20 *Stepping-Stones* (see note 9), p. 13.
21 E. Fisher, *Faith without Prejudice*, New York, 1977, p. 33.
22 M. Barth, *Jesus the Jew*, Atlanta, 1978, p. 24.
23 P. Van Buren, *Discerning the Way,* New York, 1980, p. 156.
24 R. Rendtorff in *Christian-Jewish Relations*, Vol. 16 No. 1 (March 1983), p. 18.
25 See *Black Africa and the Bible*, ed. E. Mveng and R. J. Z. Werblowsky, Jerusalem, 1972.
26 C. Klein, *Anti-Judaism in Christian Theology*, London, 1978, pp. 67-91.
27 *Ibid.*, p. 70.
28 *Ibid.*, p. 77.
29 E. Fisher, *op. cit.* (note 21), p. 26.
30 *Journal of Ecumenical Studies*, Fall 1974, p. 611.
31 *Ibid.*, p. 602.
32 A. R. Eckardt, *Elder and Younger Brothers*, New York, 1973, p. 22.
33 *Stepping Stones* (see note 10), pp. 65ff.
34 *More Stepping Stones* (see note 9), pp. 198ff.
35 *Ibid.*, pp. 207ff.
36 E. Fisher, *op.cit.* (note 21), p. 30.
37 M. Barth, *op. cit.* (note 22), p. 31.
38 R. Ruether in A. T. Davies (ed.), *op. cit.* (note 3), p. 235.
39 H. Küng in *Christian Attitudes on Jews and Judaism*, June 1977, pp. 1ff.
40 *Jewish Chronicle,* 20 December 1985, p. 21.

41 *Stepping Stones* (see note 10), pp. 1-2.

42 *More Stepping Stones* (see note 9), pp. 167ff.

43 *Stepping Stones* (see note 10), pp. 1-2.

44 E. Fisher, *op. cit.* (note 21), p. 26; *More Stepping Stones* (note 9), pp. 229-30.

45 *Stepping Stones* (note 10), pp. 91ff.

46 C. Klein, *op. cit.* (note 26), p. 112.

47 *Ibid.*, p. 97.

48 *Ibid.*, p. 112.

49 *Face to Face*, Spring 1984, p. 32.

50 G. Baum, *Jews and the Gospels*, London, 1961, and introduction to R. Ruether, *Faith and Fratricide*, New York, 1974.

51 A. R. Eckardt, *op. cit.* (note 32), pp. 54ff.

52 K. Stendahl in *Face to Face*, Fall/Winter 1977, p. 19.

53 *Twenty Years of Jewish-Catholic Relations*, ed. E. Fisher, A. J. Rudin and M. H. Tanenbaum, New York, 1986, p. 98.

54 K. Hruby in *Christians and Jews*, ed. H. Küng and W. Kasper, New York, 1974, pp. 90ff.

55 A. T. Davies, *op. cit.* (note 7), p. 114.

56 C. Klein, *op. cit.* (note 26), p. 30.

57 *Ibid.*, p. 32.

58 E. Fleischner, *op. cit.* (note 6), p. 75.

59 A. T. Davies, *op. cit.* (note 7), p. 73.

60 *Ibid.*, p. 87.

61 A. R. Eckardt, *op. cit.* (note 32), pp. 82ff.

62 E. Fleischner, *op. cit.* (note 6), p. xiv.

63 *Twenty Years*, (see note 53), pp. 171ff.

64 *Ibid.*

65 In an unpublished paper, 'The Theology of Judaism'.

66 *Christian-Jewish Relations*, No. 71, June 1980, pp.23ff.

67 *Twenty Years* (see note 53), p. 179.

68 E. Fleischner, *op. cit.* (note 6), p. 82.

69 G. Baum in R. Ruether, *op. cit.* (see note 50), p. 9.

70 A. T. Davies, *op. cit.* (note 7), p. 97.

71 C. Thoma, *op. cit.* (note 12), p. 141.

72 See C. Rijk, *op. cit.* (note 19), p. 18.

73 G. Baum in R. Ruether, *op. cit.* (note 50), p. 10.

74 J. C. Rylaarsdam, 'Two covenants and the dilemmas of Christology', *Journal of Ecumenical Studies*, Spring 1972.

75 *Stepping Stones* (note 10), p. 1ff.

76 *Ibid*, p. 60.

77 E. Fisher, *op. cit.* (note 21), p. 27.

78 G. Baum, *Christian Theology After Auschwitz*, London, 1976, p. 10.

79 *Stepping Stones* (note 10), pp. 74ff.

80 *More Stepping Stones* (note 9), pp. 167ff.

81 *Stepping Stones* (note 10), p. 133.

82 M.-T. Hoch and B. Dupuy, *Les Eglises devant le Judaïsme*, Paris, 1980, pp. 238ff.

83 *More Stepping Stones* (note 9), pp. 160ff.

84 C. Klein, *op. cit.* (note 26), p. 66.

85 R. Ruether, *op. cit.* (note 50), p. 233.
86 J. Jocz, *Christians and Jews: Encounter and Mission*, London, 1966, *passim*.
87 R. Niebuhr, *Pious and Secular America*, New York, 1958, p. 108.
88 H. H. Ditmanson in *Face to Face*, Fall/Winter 1977, pp. 6ff.
89 A. R. Eckardt in *Jewish-Christian Relations in Today's World*, ed. J. E. Wood Jr., Waco, 1971, pp. 97ff.
90 *Stepping Stones* (note 10), pp. 69ff.
91 *Ibid.*, pp. 73ff.
92 *More Stepping Stones*, (note 9), pp. 167ff.
93 J. S. Conway in *Holocaust and Genocide Studies*, Vol. 1 No. 1, 1968, pp. 138ff.
94 *More Stepping Stones* (note 9), pp. 207ff.
95 *Erwangungen zur kirchlichen Handsreichung zur Erneurung des Verhältnisses von Christen und Juden*, Evangelisch-Theologisches Seminar der Rheinisches Friedrich-Wilhelm Universität Bonn, May 1980.
96 *Stepping Stones* (note 10), pp. 147ff.
97 *Ibid.*, pp. 128ff.
98 *Christian-Jewish Relations*, Vol. 15 No. 2 (September 1983), p. 21.
99 *Christianity Today*, 4 September 1981.
100 *Christianity in Politics: The Moral Majority in the USA*, Research Report, Institute of Jewish Affairs, London, October 1982, p. 6.
101 A. R. Eckardt, *loc. cit.* (note 32), p. 12.
102 *Christian-Jewish Relations*, Vol. 16 No. 1 (March 1983), p. 22.
103 A. T. Davies, *op. cit.* (note 7), p. 42.
104 E. Borowitz, *Contemporary Christologies: A Jewish Response*, New York, 1980, p. 176.
105 R. Ruether, *op. cit.* (note 50), pp. 11ff, 227ff.
106 F. Heer, *God's First Love*, New York, 1967, p. 406.
107 See John Baker in *Theology and Racism*, London, 1985.
108 G. Baum in R. Ruether, *op. cit.* (note 50), p. 8.
109 J. B. Metz in *The Emergent Church*, New York, 1981, p. 19.
110 J. Moltmann, *The Church in the Power of the Spirit*, New York, 1977.
111 F. H. Littell, *The Crucifixion of the Jews*, New York, 1975, *passim*.
112 C. Klein, *op. cit.* (note 26), p. 13.
113 R. Everett in *Christian Attitudes on Jews and Judaism*, October 1976, pp. 10ff.
114 J. Parkes, *Prelude to Dialogue*, London, 1969, pp. 188ff.
115 See World Council of Churches' Report on Consultation on the Church and the Jewish People, 10-14 February 1986, pp. 8ff.
116 B. Martin, 'Tillich and Judaism', *Judaism*, Vol. 15, No. 2, Spring 1966, pp. 180ff.
117 R. Ruether, *op. cit.* (note 50), p. 257.
118 *Journal of Ecumenical Studies*, Fall 1974, p. 614.
119 R. Ruether, *op. cit.* (note 50), p. 257.
120 M. Barth, *op. cit.* (note 22), p. 39.
121 E. Fleischner, *op. cit.* (note 6), p. 122.
122 P. Van Buren. *op. cit.* (note 23), pp. 25ff.
123 See note 19.
124 A. R. Eckardt in S. E. Rosenberg, *The Christian Problem: A Jewish View*, New York, 1986, pp. xi-xii.

CHAPTER II

Jewish attitudes to the dialogue

Although my subject is Christian–Jewish relations since the Second World War, I must begin this chapter on Jewish attitudes with a prefatory section, as from the Jewish point of view the turning point came not with the Holocaust but with Emancipation, the emergence from the ghetto starting in the late eighteenth century. Before that time, Jews in the Christian world were often secluded behind high walls, figuratively or literally, excluded from most normal occupations, frequently subject to discrimination, persecution, attack, expulsion and massacre, depicted in demonological terms – all on the initiative of Christianity and justified in terms of Christian theology. There were certain periods and regions where the outside pressure was temporarily lowered and Jewish life flourished, but even then the position of the Jew remained inferior and a Damoclean sword was constantly poised above his head. Communication with the Christian environment on the level of equals was denied to the Jews. The source of their humiliation was the Church and under these circumstances it was too much to expect a balanced evaluation of Christianity in a Jewish milieu. Their invidious situation precluded any sober dispassionate assessment and, not surprisingly, pronouncements concerning Christianity tended to be scurrilous or apologetic. Silence was the safest course. Even when interest in Christianity was evinced, it was dangerous to speak of the faith of the persecutor. There were some exceptions and a few voices were heard which today appear progressive, but by and large the mood was hostile. In truth, the Jew was well contented to be left alone and not bothered with alien theological challenge. He remembered only too well those periods in which he had had to participate in public disputations which were not only loaded against him from the outset but conducted in categories of thought unfamiliar to his universe of discourse. So there grew up in Jewish circles a tradition of introversion which remains strong to this day among large segments of Orthodox Jews, not least in the State of Israel, and which should be seen in its historical perspective. After so many centuries of conditioning, the notable fact is not that these pockets remain, but that the attitudes of the majority have changed so radically.

Emancipation

When the Jew was allowed out of the ghetto – and we are talking primarily of central and western Europe – he could talk to the Christian for the first time on equal terms. But these conversations were often at cross-purposes. The Christian now had more opportunity to use persuasion to attract the Jew to Christianity. The Jew had his eye on social acceptance and advancement (Heine called his conversion certificate 'a passport to European civilisation' while the Bible scholar Daniel Chwolson said 'I accepted baptism out of conviction – the conviction that it is better to be a professor at the Imperial Academy in St. Petersburg than a teacher in a *heder* [small Hebrew school] in Vilna'). He also wanted to show the Christian – and also prove to himself – the validity of Judaism in a world of enlightenment. He stressed its universalistic and ethical aspects, developed Reform Judaism as a response to the challenges of the open society, and built monumental synagogues prominently displaying a universal symbol – the tablets of the decalogue.

In face of the ideological challenge of Christianity, the first reaction was polemic, albeit of a refined nature, attacking Christian ideology. In many ways this was an extension of the traditional apologetics, but now with new angles. Christianity loomed not as a threat but as a temptation. However, it could now be subject to analysis free of artificial external pressures. The challenge was to demonstrate to the emancipated Jew the superiority of Judaism in contemporary categories. The enlightened Jewish thinkers of the nineteenth century, such as the Germans, Samuel Hirsch, Solomon Formstecher and Solomon Steinheim, sought to prove the superiority of Judaism over Christianity, although at the same time they allotted to Christianity an honoured, if lesser, place. In particular, they singled out and attacked what they discerned as pagan elements in Christianity, amongst which they numbered transsubstantiation, the cult of relics, the institution of sainthood, and even the doctrine of the Trinity. The pioneer of Reform in the United States, Isaac Mayer Wise, concluded: 'The New Testament is the fulfilment of the Old only by the grace of the Church and the bookbinder.'[1]

Under the circumstances, the polemics were inevitable, but noteworthy is the emergence of a new element of understanding, even appreciation, if somewhat begrudging, of the contribution of Christianity which from its position of power had disseminated monotheism and a Jewish-style ethic to the world, for the eventual triumph of the parent – and purer – religion. Thus Formstecher characterised Christianity and Islam as the northern and southern missions of Judaism to the pagan world while the Italian thinker, Elijah Benamozegh, wrote 'We admire these children of ours' although he qualifed his positive comments, writing that he found it inconceivable that God should reject one form of morality for another. The seeds for this development of greater understanding had already been sown in the late eighteenth century by the pioneer of Emancipation, Moses Mendelssohn. He attempted to find ways to bridge the gaps between the mutual perceptions of the two faiths and declared his readiness to acknowledge the innocence and goodness of Jesus on condition that: (a) he never meant to regard himself as equal with the Father; (b) he never proclaimed himself as a person of divinity; (c) he never presumptuously claimed the honour of worship; and (d) he did not intend to subvert the faith of his fathers.[2] He complained that quarrels between Judaism and Christianity merely lead to the general weakening of religion – a theme that was to re-emerge after the Second World War. To quote Mendelssohn's noble words:

It is unbecoming for one of us to openly defy the other and thereby furnish diversion to the idle, scandal to the simple and malicious exultation to the revilers of truth and virtue. Were we to analyse our aggregate stock of knowledge, we certainly shall concur in so many important truths that I venture to say few individuals of one and the same religious persuasion would more harmonise in thinking. A point here and there on which we might perhaps still divide might be adjourned for some ages longer, without detriment to the welfare of the human race. What a world of bliss we would live in did all men adopt the true principles which the best among the Christians and the best among the Jews have in common.

What a path of thorns and blood had to be trodden before this was taken up seriously. Unfortunately these feelers evoked no response on the Christian side which took no action to mitigate anti-Semitism, while continuing its missionary activities.

The twentieth century

It has been said that up to the Second World War, Jews and Christians engaged not in dialogue but in double monologue. Christians wanted to prove the superiority of their faith; Jews were primarily concerned with bettering their lot in society. Christians wanted converts; Jews, civil rights. Jews were forced to talk religion where they meant social betterment.[3]

However, as we move into the twentieth century, the breakthrough on the Jewish side becomes even more pronounced, still spearheaded – ironically, we can say with the advantage of hindsight – by German Jews. At this time, Jewish thinkers seeking an affinity with Christianity were necessarily confined to the world of Protestantism. The Catholic world had not changed, while the Jewish masses in eastern Europe, accounting for the overwhelming majority of world Jewry, had not achieved Emancipation and were still subject to the traditional intolerance of the Catholic and Orthodox Churches.

The influential early twentieth century philosopher, Hermann Cohen, wrote extensive critiques of Christianity but nevertheless sensed a deep relation between Judaism and Christianity, especially in its Protestant manifestations, with their emphasis on the believing individual. The bond between Judaism and Christianity is to be sought in the life of reason, which Judaism has attained in greater measure. Jewish scholars now began to turn their attention to the figures of Jesus and Paul, bringing Jewish scholarship to bear on analyses of the New Testament and the emergence of Christianity. On occasion they tended to re-create Jesus to correspond to their own ideology – to Claude Montefiore he was a Liberal Jew, to Joseph Klausner, a Jewish nationalist – but in any case the Jewishness of Jesus, the apostles and the Gospels were now increasingly expounded.

The seminal figures in the evolution of modern Jewish attitudes to Christianity culminating in the dialogue are Franz Rosenzweig and Martin Buber, writing around the 1920s. Rosenzweig pioneered the construction of a relationship without polemic, seeing Christianity as a possible way to the truth, although, like any committed thinker, he saw the ultimate truth in his own faith. He was the first Jewish theologian to view Christianity as equally legitimate as Judaism, both having their origin in the Divine. He proposed the doctrine of the Two Covenants which in a mysterious way stand united before God. The first covenant is with the people of Israel and establishes their existence as God's people: through the covenant the Jews are already with the Father. Christianity is the Judaism of the Gentiles and through it the nations of the world establish their relationship with the Divine. The vocation of Christianity is to bring the nations of the world to the covenant. On this basis, Judaism and Christianity can recognise the integrity of the other, asking for understanding, not change. At the end of time they will be united, but meanwhile neither religion must attempt to adopt the path of the other. Christianity, then, is on its way to its goal, but Judaism has arrived. A Christian has to become a Christian – he is born a heathen; a Jew is born a Jew. Rosenzweig felt that eventually it would be Christianity that would change. Jesus would lose his significance – he is a necessary intermediary for Gentiles but not needed by the Jews. Both faiths are true, both are required in the Divine plan and the wall between the two will only be broken at the end of time, when Christianity would become Jewish.

Buber, like Rosenzweig, felt that we can acknowledge as a

mystery that which someone else confesses as the reality of his faith, even though it opposes our own knowledge. This implied the reality of Christianity as a path to God and the demand that Christianity recognise Judaism as a path to God. It also involves rejection of the Christian claim to a monopoly on the path to salvation. Buber distinguished between two types of faith: *emuna*, the biblical pattern, which was the faith of Jesus, and the Greek *pistis*, followed by Paul. The faith of Jesus was broad, dealing with the problems of all people, that of Paul was chiefly interested in the individual and in human salvation through Christ. Buber felt that Christianity required a change of emphasis from *pistis* to *emuna*. The Jew carries the burden of the unredeemed world. He knows that redemption is not an accomplished fact and knows of no redeemer who has appeared at one point in history to inaugurate a new and redeemed history. We Jews, he wrote, do not perceive any caesura in history, no midpoint, but only a goal – the goal of the way to God, and do not pause on our way. At the same time he allows for the possibility that God may have revealed himself to Jesus but cannot ascribe finality to any of his revelations nor to anyone the character of the incarnation. To Buber it was justification by faith which separated Judaism from Christianity. Nevertheless he looked forward to the time when the Jews would recognise Jesus as a great religious figure, calls Jesus 'my brother', and insists that the gates of God are open to all. The Christian need not go through Judaism nor the Jew through Christianity to come to God. No-one outside Israel can understand the mystery of Israel and no-one outside Christianity can understand the mystery of Christendom. 'How can the mysteries stand side by side? That is God's mystery.' Buber also ascribes great importance to the role of Jewish peoplehood in the Jewish religion and sees this as part of the Jewish theological mainstream which finds in the link between the people and religion one of the main points of distinction between Judaism and Christianity.

Finally in this introductory section, I would mention another German thinker, the Reform rabbi, Leo Baeck. His best-known contribution on the subject was his characterisation of Judaism as a classic religion and Christianity as a romantic religion. Defining romantic religion he wrote: 'Tense feelings supply its contents and it seeks its goals in the now mythical, now mystical visions of the imagination. Its world is the world of the irregular, the extraordinary and the miraculous, that world which lies beyond all reality.' For the romantic, the impression, the mood is everything – to illustrate which he cites Paul taking faith, revelation and ecstasy as the ultimate fulfilment of religion. The romantically pious does not go beyond feeling and prayer. In classical religion demands are made; in romantic religion, all is given. The only activity of the genuinely romantic is self-congratulation on the act of grace. In classical religion, man is to become free through the commandments; in romantic religion, he becomes free through grace. Veracity and justice as active virtues have no place in romanticism and from here the step to active intolerance is small. Baeck, like the others we have mentioned, was seeking a Jewish understanding of Christianity but without whitewashing or blurring of differences or any attempt at syncretism. The great innovation already reached in this pre-war Jewish thinking is the teaching that the other way – or surely, other ways – concerning which we will continue to have our reservations, can also culminate in truth.

After the Holocaust

Jewish thinkers such as Rosenzweig, Buber and Baeck were ahead of Christian thinkers of their time in their gropings towards mutual theological understanding. It needed the trauma of the Holocaust to shock Christian thinkers into a parallel awareness. In reading the optimistic evaluation of mankind that came from these pre-war Jewish thinkers – and remember that most of it emanated from Germany – we can realise that Jewish optimism can be taken too far. When we emerge from the tunnel of the Holocaust, Jewish thinkers are convinced that Nazi anti-Semitism would have been unthinkable without the conditioning of centuries of Christian anti-Semitism, which paved the way for its acceptability among the European Christian masses. Yet the Holocaust, while introducing a fresh and grim perspective, dimmed but did not completely obliterate the basic Jewish theology of hope. Martin Buber arrived in Palestine a refugee. Leo Baeck passed the last two years of the war in the notorious Theresienstadt concentration camp. Jews everywhere wrestled with the problem 'Where was God in Auschwitz?' Yet even as these realities were being faced, the search for understanding continued. Many Jews welcomed the new perceptions and attitudes developing in Christian circles with their realisation of the perniciousness of traditional doctrines, and hoped for a phoenix of reconciliation to rise from the ashes of the Holocaust. Theological grounds were cited to criticise the new relationship but only a minority took the lesson of the Holocaust to the extreme conclusion that it rendered dialogue impossible.

One such completely negative voice – the most outspoken critic of dialogue – has been Eliezer Berkovits, an Orthodox thinker who originally came to England as a refugee from Nazism. To him, the age of Christian militancy is over and we are living in a post-Christian world. It is the new revolutionary distribution of the balance of power that accounts for today's Christian ecumenism. Christians now speak of freedom of religion because they are interested in freedom for Christians, notably in communist lands, and intolerance is for them no longer a viable option. Christians must, willy-nilly, now fall back on persuasion and all friendly statements should be seen in this light. He writes of the moral bankruptcy of Christian civilisation and the spiritual bankruptcy of the Christian religion, citing the extermination of six million Jews, one and a half million of whom were children, in the very heart of Christian Europe, accompanied by the criminal silence of virtually all Christians, including that of a Holy Father in Rome, as the culmination of this bankruptcy. At this stage, it is emotionally impossible to enter into a dialogue, which in any case is fruitless and pointless in a theological sense. The New Testament he sees as the most dangerous anti- Semitic tract in history which has poisoned the hearts of millions over two millenia. Before anything, he writes, we must face the truth of Christian criminality against the Jewish people.[4] The Christian crime against the Jewish people he characterises as the devil's laughter at all those nice Christian affirmations about turning the other cheek and loving one's enemy.[5] This may be strong stuff, but his sarcastic comments on the discovery that the Jews are not an accursed people or that they require some sort of absolution for an imaginary deicide evoke a wide echo in Jewish circles.

A strongly critical, if somewhat more temperate, attack on Christian historical guilt and its role in the Holocaust marks the views of other thinkers. We have mentioned Jules Isaac (p. 4) whose exposition of the Christian 'teaching of contempt' towards the Jews down the ages found a responsive ear in certain Christian circles, notably in the Vatican.[6] For Ignaz Maybaum, a Reform rabbi who fled to England as a refugee from Germany, Auschwitz is not unique in Jewish history but the reappearance of a classic and sanctified event. He understood the message of the Crucifixion as that someone had to die that others may live, and thus the modern Jew collectively, as the single Jew many centuries ago, must mount the Cross, i.e. undergo persecution and death, in order to arouse the conscience of the Gentile world. In Auschwitz, Jews suffered vicarious atonement for the sins of mankind; it was the Golgotha of modern man. However, he did not despair and found encouragement in the new relationship inaugurated by the Vatican Declaration on the Jews and felt that after Auschwitz, both Jew and Christian can go beyond the historic postures of their medieval period to a reformed post-Holocaust future.[7]

Emil Fackenheim, also of German origin and himself for a time in a concentration camp, has also wrestled with the question of the Holocaust and Christian responsibility. For him, the main lesson to be learnt from the Holocaust is to survive, and he formulates for the contemporary Jew a new commandment – it is forbidden to hand Hitler a posthumous victory.[8] He writes that for Christians the first priority today must be theological self-understanding; for Jews it is – and after Auschwitz must be – simple safety for their children.[9] The Christian, for his part, has a special obligation to recognise and support the vitality of the Jewish people – this is the least he can do. Historic changes have indeed occurred in post-war Western Christian attitudes but organised Christianity will find it easiest to drop the ancient charge of deicide, harder to recognise the anti-Semitic roots of the New Testament, and hardest of all to face up to the fact that Jews and Judaism are both still alive. How can a Jew, he asks, however he may strain his ears, hear God speak to the Christian church if, even after Auschwitz, the ancient calumny of the fossilisation of Judaism is not totally rejected? For Fackenheim, the great positive message that has emerged from God is the rebirth of the State of Israel, symbol of hope and survival for the Jewish people. He feels that in Israel's hours of danger, in 1967 and 1973, the Church abandoned the Jews even though they faced a second Holocaust, because it still cannot face the fact of the first. The ultimate root of the Christian rejection of Judaism lies in the view, which continues to linger even where Christianity is undermined by atheism or agnosticism, that the faith of Christianity as the New Israel entails the death of the old. To hold this belief continues Hitler's work.[10]

Another Jewish thinker who has devoted much thought to the implications of the Holocaust is the American Orthodox rabbi, Irving Greenberg who, unlike the others previously mentioned, belongs to a younger generation and had no direct experience of the tragedy. He writes of revelatory–oriented events that occur in history which bring humans into a reality beyond themselves. Such events set the goals and direction of the religion, and the retelling or re-enactment of the orienting event is the central liturgical act of the religion. This century has seen both for Jews and Christians two orienting events: the Holocaust and the rebirth of Israel. Crucifixion and resurrection have recurred in this generation. Both Judaism and Christianity are religions of redemption; both proclaim a God who cares about the preciousness of the human in the image of God. The Holocaust is a total assault on such a belief. It undercuts the persuasiveness of both religions and contradicts the hope they offer. The implications of Christian anti-Semitism and of Christian silence strike further at the claims of religion. We cannot go on as if nothing has happened. The Holocaust must be a major event in Christian history and Christianity will not be able to overcome its legacy of guilt without a major purging of the sources of Jew-hatred. This calls for a head-on confrontation with the Gospels and the Church Fathers' tradition of supersessionism and anti-Semitism. It means the realisation that the process of redemption is far less advanced than Christians had assumed, together with a new emphasis on worldly redemption, personal responsibility and human creativity. He believes that this would evoke a Jewish response which would recognise the authenticity of a Christian responsibility and acknowledge the legitimacy of the Christian unfolding as long as it does not destroy or deny the unfailing life of the Jewish covenant.[11]

The Israeli thinker, Uriel Tal, distinguished between the Christian and the pagan un-Christian elements active in modern anti-Semitism from its inception, with their contribution to the Holocaust. He quotes Freud who, in his *Moses and Monotheism*, suggested that modern anti-Semitism should be seen in the light of a rebellion against Christianity of its pre-Christian pagan heritage. This applied chiefly to those historical areas of civilisation where Christianity was imposed upon idolatrous nations by force. In modern political and racist anti-Semitism he discerns a negation not only of Judaism but also of Christianity, which was interpreted as continuing or even developing the essential defects of Judaism. Both religions were seen as alienating man from his authentic primal nature and sapping his natural physical vitality. Both imprison the spirit and body of man in chains of abstract rationalistic moral rules. Judaism then is negated as the prototype of anti-pagan forces, such as monotheism and Christianity. As a lesson of the Holocaust, the realisation is beginning to dawn that racist anti-Semitism saw its ideal not only in destroying the Jews, but also in destroying Judaism as a symbol of culture and of history based on spiritual principles and accordingly also on the Jewish heritage included in Christianity.[12]

While it is impossible to generalise concerning the conclusions drawn from the Holocaust experience by Jewish thinkers – in general theological attitudes as well as affecting Jewish–Christian relations – I have selected representative responses. What must always be remembered is that the Holocaust trauma has entered the subconscious of every Jew, however apparently remote from Judaism, and – whether given explicit expression or not – it informs all Jewish encounters with Christianity and Christians in the post-war world. It remains doubtful whether the recognition of this development has penetrated as deeply in Christian thinking as is called for. The fact that the latest Vatican document on relations with the Jews, the 1985 'Notes', dismissed the Holocaust almost as an aside came as a shock and a surprise to Jews who thought that at least the profound significance of this experience for Jews had been understood by their dialogue partners.

Jewish expectations of Christian attitudes

Where there is agreement among Jewish thinkers is that, despite the progress that has been made, the seeds of anti-Semitism have been left in place in Christian thinking. As long as it is taught, explicitly or implicitly, that Jews (even if not all Jews) were responsible for the death of Jesus, that in the eyes of God Judaism has been replaced by Christianity, that the Old Testament has been outdated by and only finds meaning in the New Testament, that since the time of Jesus the Jews have been the objects, not the subjects, of history – the teaching of contempt, with all that flows from it, continues.

The aspect of Jews as the subjects of history brings us to the second basic event in recent Jewish history – the rebirth of the State of Israel, described by some as the return of the Jews to history. In Chapter IV, I will consider the attitudes of Christian churches to this development; here I wish to refer to Jewish expectations of Christian attitudes.

Religious Jews are themselves theologically divided concerning the significance of the event. To the more extreme fundamentalist Jews it is even a non-event, as it has occurred under secular auspices, unaccompanied by Messianic manifestations; the less extreme Orthodox are divided as to whether or not it should be seen as the beginning of the promised Divine redemption. But for the great majority it constitutes a historic watershed and must doubtlessly be taken into consideration as a key element in contemporary Jewish self-definition. The survival of the State of Israel is critical to Jews today, those of faith and those of no religious faith. Moreover, despite its apparent strength, the frequent calls for its destruction among certain Arab circles coupled with the Holocaust consciousness just mentioned combine to leave sufficient of a question-mark over its long-term prospects to engender attitudes of desparate determination in many Jewish circles that are not always easily fathomable by the outsider. In a dialogue context this calls for the Christian recognition of just how deeply Israel is etched on the Jewish soul, not always an easy demand to meet as this land identification is alien to Christians as a religious concept.

In the words of the British Chief Rabbi, Sir Immanuel Jakobovits:

> In the self-definition of Judaism a major impact is bound to be made by the restoration of Jewish sovereignty. Any redefinition of Church attitudes to the Jewish people which leaves this fundamental change out of account is incomplete. Quite irrelevant are differences of opinion over particular Israeli governmental policies. We seek recognition of Israel's legitimacy and its right to a secure existence.[13]

Rabbi Henry Siegman, a leading American participant in the dialogue, has written that:

> Even if Israel were to pose a political rather than a theological problem, the warmest theological friendships would be meaningless and utterly without human content if they could contemplate the collapse of Israel with equanimity. But in fact, Israel presents not only a political issue but has the profoundest theological implications. The State of Israel is the result not only of modern forces of nationalism or even of persecution but is the actualisation of a quest for authenticity.[14]

Opposition to Israel deriving from the Christian Left is a growth of the past two decades which has caused great concern in Jewish circles. Many Jews characterise Christian anti-Zionism as the current manifestation of Christian anti-Semitism. Anti-Semitism is out of fashion since the Holocaust but the anti-Semites can regroup under the banner of anti-Zionism, not in the sense of criticism of a specific policy of an Israeli government but as the denial of Israel's very right to exist as a Jewish state, expressed through attempts at delegitimation – at this stage primarily in international fora – and of the right of the Jewish people to a national territorial expression in the Land of Israel. The most notorious success of these forces was the United Nations 1975 resolution equating Zionism with racism. To return to Siegman, he finds in this attitude a peculiar blend of an uncritical celebration of the Third World and a theological anti-Semitism that is nourished by a Christian universalism which cannot abide the earthiness of Jewish particularism; they love Jews who are disincarnated suffering servants but cannot abide Jews who are flesh and blood people, who need to occupy physical space in a real world before they fulfil whatever loftier aspirations they may have.[15]

Orthodox Jewish reactions

I have described (p. 55) Berkovits's rejection of dialogue in the shadow of the Holocaust. His is not the only critical attitude. The more extreme Orthodox, like other fundamentalists, do not countenance dialogue on principle although they support coexistence for pragmatic reasons. The more moderate Orthodox also have theological reservations and have restricted the scope of their participation. Their attitude has been dictated by the views of their authoritative leaders, notably the American rabbi Joseph Dov Soloveichik. His basic premise is that faith communities must inevitably find it impossible to communicate with each other, except on what he calls 'secular grounds' or 'human categories'. The Jewish community must always be mindful of the mystery of the uniqueness of its being and must not expose the inner life of its faith to interreligious dialogue. The universal and the covenantal are mutually exclusive. Each faith community has its own individuality and faith imperatives and commandments cannot be equated with the ritual and ethics of another community. It is futile to seek common denominators and each faith believes that its own system of values is for the ultimate good and must therefore be unyielding. At the same time there is no contradiction in co-ordinating *cultural activity* with all men while confronting them as another faith community. Such confrontation requires equal rights and full religious freedom, with no attitude of superiority on either side. Thus we can talk together as historians and sociologists of religion but the only way we can talk to each other theologically would be by renouncing our faith.[16]

These views are echoed in Chief Rabbi Jakobovits's assertion that what we do not seek are theological dialogues in the narrow sense of subjecting each faith to the critical scrutiny of the other nor do we aspire to joint religious services or to interfaith activities of a specifically interreligious nature. 'We regard our relationship with God and the manner in which we define it and collectively express it as being so intimate and personal that we would no more convey it to outsiders than we would share with others our husband-wife relationship', he has written.[17]

Jews in the dialogue

Among Jews, then, the response to the Christian outreach has been divided. The Orthodox Rabbinical Council of America laid down guidelines according to the views of Rabbi Soloveichik, welcoming discussions of universal religious problems but reject-ing debate of 'our private individual commitment' or, as some put it, excluding from dialogue the consideration of 'truth'. They were ready for dialogue, and even felt it essential, on topics dealing with the 'religious–spiritual aspects of our civilisation' – for exam-ple, war and peace, secularism, civil rights and moral values – but rejected interreligious dialogue concerning the 'doctrinal, dog-matic or ritual aspects of our faith. . . There cannot be mutual understanding concerning these topics, for Jews and Christians will employ different categories and move within incommensu-rate frames of reference and evaluation.'[18]

On the other hand, Jews of the Progressive trends (Liberal and Reform in Britain, corresponding to Reform and Conservative in the US) as well as Jewish academic scholars have been deeply involved in theological dialogue. For some it is plain good sense to seize a historical opportunity and move into an era of dialogue. Some have been motivated by belief in a Jewish mission to bring at least a social and ethical message to the widest possible public. For some the consideration is that all men of faith are threatened by the spread of pagan secularism and need to stand together in face of common danger, and this would also be echoed in certain Orthodox circles. In the words of Chief Rabbi Jakobovits: 'The danger to Judaism is not in the allurement of baptism but in the threat of indifference in a pagan society.'[19]

In fact, the distinction drawn by Orthodox thinkers concerning 'theological' dialogue is elusive as Jewish faith is so broad and inclusive that it is difficult to draw lines. In Judaism, the aspects of faith, ritual, the ethical and the social are so intertwined as to be inextricable. Indeed this very oneness is the glory of Judaism. Certainly many dialogues have been held in which the subject has been carefully staked out so as not to offend Orthodox susceptibilities but have inevitably and sometimes imperceptibly entered these forbidden territories.

In any case, the lack of symmetry in the Jewish–Christian relationship and an imbalance in expectations should be noted. For the Jews, Christianity does not pose a theological problem and Jewish participation in the dialogue does not have the same level of theological motivation as among the Christians, and often is entered into for the sake of the Christian partners. For the Christians involved, their very Christianity grew out of Judaism and indeed depends on it; for the Jews there is no relationship of dependency or causality. One recalls that when Franz Rosenzweig was asked what the Jews thought of Jesus, he replied 'They don't.' Jewish interests in the dialogue tend to be more pragmatic, their considerations are often historical rather than theological, and directed to the safeguarding of Jewish positions in societies that are at least nominally Christian. High on their list of priorities is the hope for Christian recognition that anti-Semitism is not integral but a discardable accretion. However, they are having to face new challenges, as has been pointed out by the Israeli philosopher, Natan Rotenstreich. In the past, they concentrated on self-interpretation and were preoccupied with systems of ideas, not living patterns of culture. To meet the challenge of Christian thought and establish Judaism on solid theoretical foundations, Jewish thinkers are now forced to deal with the world of non-Jewish ideas.[20]

The influential American Jewish thinker and dialogue pioneer, Abraham Joshua Heschel, noted three factors as influencing Jewish–Christian relations in our day: the Holocaust in a civilisation that was nominally Christian; the rapid spread of secularism and nihilism in a world that repudiates the Biblical message; and the Hebrew Bible as a common patrimony of Jews and Christians.[21] As we have noted, in fact both sides read the Hebrew Bible differently but, increasingly, both sides are getting back to an understanding of the Hebrew Bible unencumbered by layers of tradition, and this bodes well for the future. At present, however, it is as misleading to speak of a common Bible legacy as it is of a Judeo–Christian tradition. One of the conditions placed by Soloveichik for dialogue is to beware of speaking of any 'common trend' except in a historic-cultural context. It has become usual in the Western world, especially the United States, to speak of the 'Judeo–Christian tradition' (in Europe, the term 'Jewish–Christian amity' is more frequently heard). In Chapter I, we mentioned some Christian views (see pp. 41-2). The concept is used in certain Jewish circles, along the lines laid down by the US Reform Jewish theologian Eugene Borowitz who warns: 'a secularism unguided by Christianity and paying no attention to its handful of believing Jews would become a new paganism, one far more dangerous than anything the prophets and rabbis fought against – Judaism has far more in common with Christianity than with a secularism gone pagan'.[22] His conclusion is that the secularist enemy can bring the two faiths together. The campaign will be more effective if the allies can achieve a broad basis of strategic agreement between them. This calls for a common language which can be summed up in the designation 'Judeo–Christian tradition'. Many Jewish thinkers, and not only in Orthodox circles, have rejected the concept. Thus the American writer Arthur A. Cohen wrote a book entitled *The Myth of the Judeo–Christian Tradition*, in which he states that less than a tradition of continuity between Jews and Christians is a tradition of enmity and suspicion. It is to be hoped in time that Judeo–Christian enmity will be transformed into Judeo–Christian humanism, but never a Judeo–Christian tradition. The goal should be unanimity, not unity.

Cohen traces the trend to speak of a 'Judeo–Christian tradition' back to the Enlightenment when the connection was made by men such as Voltaire, opposed to *both* traditions. Jewish scholars of the nineteenth century, as we have seen, began to suggest that the doctrine of Jesus was a perpetuation of Judaism but even the more liberal never saw Christian theology as meaningful or demanding. Cohen himself is deeply offended by Christianity's attitude of condescension to the House of Israel. Whether Judaism is conceived as an arrested child or an aged father, the Church's image of solicitude cloaks a refined triumphalism and the Jew remains a mere object of action.

The Judeo–Christian myth, says Cohen, is a projection of the will to endure before a world that regards both traditions as irrelevant and meaningless. But how can we talk of a common tradition where we are divided so basically? Where Christianity assumes fulfilment, Judaism denies it. Where Christianity affirms the completion of history (or at least the accomplishment of that instrument whereby history, in God's time, may be completed), Judaism insists on the unredeemed character of history.[23] Further basic differences are cited by other writers, Jewish and Christian, who have attacked the concept of commonalty.

An extreme view is held by Yeshayahu Leibowitz, a maverick Israeli thinker. To him there was never any common Judeo–Christian heritage because Christianity could not be said to have emerged from Judaism as it is its negation. It did not draw from Jewish soil or religion or practice – the Torah or commandments – but was an outgrowth of Hellenism in its last stages of degeneration with the then popular religious syncretism. Gilbert Murray, he writes, discerned five stages of Greek religion; Christianity was the sixth, springing from Middle Eastern paganism. The real challenge to the Church, he holds, is not the Crucifixion but the continuing existence of the Jewish people which is a contradiction of Christianity. Leibowitz, by the way, maintains that it is impossible to know anything about the historical Jesus, whom he suspects is the creation of the mythological imagination. In any case his only interest in the Christian conception of Jesus is because of its impact on Jewish history and fate.[24]

Here I would like to note, parenthetically, that we are all too often divided by semantics. For one thing, Christian terminology is pejoratively slanted against Judaism. Compare the traditional association with Judaism of 'obsolescence', 'legalism', 'particularism', 'judgement', 'letter of the law', as against 'love', 'grace', 'universalism', 'spirit' associated with Christianity. Look in a dictionary and you will find 'Christian' is a synonym for 'humanitarian', 'Jew' for 'miser', 'cheat'. We are also sometimes separated by our different usages of the same terms. Judaism developed in a Hebraic–Semitic world; Christianity in a Greco–Latin universe. Thought patterns and directions differed, and as the two groups have come to the dialogue they have found their differences accentuated by linguistic usage. Thus in the English-speaking world, Christians and Jews have had to find terms in English for theological concepts forged in other languages. These concepts may be far from congruent in the original but in English they are represented by the same term. The Greek *nomos* and the Hebrew *Torah* and *halacha*, for instance, are all translated as 'law'. The Christian *pistis* and the Jewish *emuna* are both translated as 'faith'. 'Secularism' is not the same for the Jew as for the Christian inasmuch as Christianity is a totally religious concept, whereas for Judaism the parameters are not necessarily religious. There are many unique terms for which there is no adequate English translation – such as *Torah* or *teshuva* in Hebrew or *agape* in Greek. Often, in dialogue, we are talking at cross-purposes.

Jews and the Christian mission

In the previous chapter, mention was made of Christian views on mission to the Jews, an issue central to Jews. There are those who have expressed the fear that the Church is now trying to accomplish through love and persuasion what it failed over the centuries to achieve by threats and force. And no church has renounced the at least implicit hope for Jewish conversion. While some continue to maintain active mission to the Jews, Jewish sensitivities on this matter are not confined to the Orthodox. Progressive Jews, too, looking for a formula for what has been called the theology of equality, are offended by missionary activity and, even when that has been suppressed, the retention of a conversionist mentality. For the Jews, the very integrity of the dialogue depends on the cessation of all Christian attempts to make Jews the objects of mission. There are still churches, especially Protestant ones, who insist that 'ultimate truth' cannot be excluded even in a dialogue situation, while notwithstanding the modification or discarding of traditional mission, many Jews continue to suspect a hidden agenda. In fact, it would be unrealistic not to recognise that some such agenda is inevitable – and on both sides. The Christian, whose faith is based on the belief that Jesus is the key to salvation and redemption, must live in the hope that this will eventually be accepted by all mankind – not least by the Jews as God's first chosen people, referred to recently by the Pope as 'our elder brothers'. So that even if active mission in this direction is renounced, the hope – at least – is built into Christian eschatology. And while Jewish eschatological expectation does not anticipate that the whole world will – or needs to – embrace Judaism, it does foresee the nations of the world recognising Israel as the people of God and its message as of universal validity. In such a scheme, Christianity would retain a role but the triumph is that of Judaism. Any believer must by definition be convinced of the superiority of his faith so that then logically any other faith must somehow be inferior. The great voices of dialogue have tried to construct schemae based on the concept of parallel lines or complementary revelations The eventual showdown is often postponed to the end of days, which is a useful theological cop-out. I am reminded of a statement by the Jerusalem New Testament scholar, David Flusser, to a group of visiting Evangelicals: 'Why should we let ourselves be involved in dispute and controversy? After all, you believe in the Messiah and we believe in the Messiah. So let us both work and pray for his coming. But when he does arrive, permit me to ask him one question: "Excuse me, sir, but is this your first visit to Jerusalem?"'

The Reform theologian, Jakob J. Petuchowski, has put it this way:

> While I as a Jew have no right to demand from my Christian neighbour that he give up an essential part of his religious obligation in order to suit my Jewish convenience, I would plead with him to have some regard for both historical realities and the power of God. I would point out to him the rather meagre harvest in Jewish souls which the Church has been able to reap since it started its mission to the Jews some two thousand years ago; and I would raise the question whether the present time holds out more hope for success than all previous times have done. I would suggest that bringing about the eschaton is a task to be shared by both God and man; and I would raise the question whether, even from a Christian perspective, the ultimate conversion of the Jews might not well be an act which God has reserved to Himself?[25]

Henry Siegman has put forward challenging views on mission. He too notes the absence of voluntary converts from Judaism; even these were usually attracted by economic and social opportunities which are no longer factors coming into play. But still, he says, if those talking to each other have given up in advance any intention, hope or desire of convincing the other, what is the point of dialogue? If Jews ask Christians to renounce any hope of converting Jews, does not this mean that we are willing to talk only to those Christians who are less secure in their faith than we are in ours? We should avoid dialogue with Christians for whom Judaism is a lifeless fossil – this is a useless exercise. But honest and respectful relations are possible with those who see present-day Judaism as an expression of Divine providence while claiming for Christianity a greater degree of truth. If we Jews demand Christian understanding of our own self-definition, we must give considerable consideration to Christian self-definition which includes the mandate to go forth and spread the truth of Christianity. Witness is a legitimate religious enterprise as long as it fully respects the freedom of conscience of men of other faiths.[26]

A Jewish statement on Christianity?

Various statements on Jews and Judaism from churches have been quoted. Now Christian circles are beginning to ask: 'Why not a Jewish statement about Christianity and the Church?' Thus Father John Pawlikowski has written recently that what is required is a step from the Jews – the creation of a consensus statement on whether Christianity in any way represents a covenantal moment from the Jewish faith perspective.

> I think it is vital for Jews to have some concrete experience in writing a consensus document of this kind so that there might be better appreciation of the difficulties involved. Also Jews cannot continue critiquing the Church's theological approach to Judaism without an equal opportunity for Christians to do the same with a Jewish statement.[27]

Jewish rethinking of the contribution Christianity might make to this self-understanding is in its infancy, he complains. A growing number of scholars do see a potential contribution although some continue to maintain that Christianity has nothing to add to Jewish insights about human religiosity. In general, Jewish scholars have not gone as far as Christians in reformulating their stance concerning the other, and they are also behind in formulating theological principles for religious pluralism.[28] This is not a lone voice from the Christian world. The Bible scholar Lawrence Boadt writes:

> Some hard questions must be asked of the Jews for this to be a mutual enterprise. Can Jews recognise a place for Christianity as a legitimate extension of the first covenant? Is the unity of the community of faith so central that no offshoots may be allowed to develop along separate paths? Was the end of the diversity represented by the Jewish 'sects' of the first century the authoritative end of all permissible diversity in the expression of covenant community? Still ahead lies intensive discussion of the Noahide commandments in Jewish tradition as a way for the Gentiles. Much work on covenant bonds between Jews and Christians remains to be done.[29]

Bishop Jorge Mejia told Jews marking the twentieth anniversary of *Nostra Aetate* in Rome that he hoped the Jews would come up with parallel projects to help Jews better understand Christianity. He realised that this was a theological task but affirmed that he could not see how theology could be avoided when talking about Christian doctrinal issues.

It is impractical to expect a Jewish consensus on the subject. It is almost impossible to expect a Jewish consensus on any subject, certainly of a religious nature. It may also be asked just how much of a consensus do the Christian statements represent. The World Council of Churches with over 300 churches, can reach a consensus of sorts on a restricted number of issues. A case in point was its 1983 Declaration on Christian–Jewish Relations, which was considerably whittled down after its initial formulation and then not brought before the General Assembly of the World Council of Churches for fear of its divisive implications and the absence of a real consensus. In any case an overall Christian statement on Jews – and probably any other subject – representing Catholic, Protestant (including Evangelical) and Orthodox Churches would be unthinkable. So would be a consensual Jewish statement in view of the deep differences among the various trends. It may be possible to ask some of these individual groups or thinkers to grapple with the question. To quote Siegman again:

> Taking full advantage of the perquisites of the injured party, Jews have successfully managed the dialogue so that it has focused entirely on what we consider to be Christian failings; we have not been compelled to examine ourselves and the problematics of our own theology and traditions – at least not within the context of the dialogue. I suppose that Christian forebearance with this one-sided situation is compounded of a state of guilt and of noblesse oblige. However, this is not likely to persist for long, not only because our Christian partners are not likely to continue the dialogue under these circumstances but because of the Jewish need to come to terms with the implications of their own traditions for a meaningful pluralism.[30]

Another noted US practitioner of the dialogue, Rabbi Mark Tanenbaum, has reached a similar conclusion:

> The bewildering and bewildered response of many Jews to Vatican

Council II with their attitudes towards present-day Christians based on old-world memories of Christian as persecutors, threw into sharp relief the critical need for Jews to develop a theology of Christians and Christianity that is consonant with the realities of an emerging 'new Christian' society that is struggling in unparallelled fashion to uproot anti-Semitism and to restore her traditions to biblical modes of thought and practise.[31]

Not all Jews agree. There are those who say that the Christian need to reconsider its attitudes to Judaism results from its inner theological links with Judaism and its belated sense of guilt for historical wrongs – neither of which apply to Judaism. But while no consensus can be expected, statements by individuals or restricted groups may be forthcoming. Thus the Conservative rabbi, Mordecai Waxman, feels that operative guidelines can be issued, even if not reduced to formal statements. Jews cannot accept that Christianity came by the will of God as the successor of Judaism, that salvation comes through belief in Jesus or that the New Testament is a new revelation. But following medieval authorities, it can be recognised that Christianity is a religion fulfilling monotheistic principles and in its own way leading to the Messiah. The two can live in harmony with no need to seek to convert Christians. This calls for a parallel view of Judaism by Christians.[32]

The Reform rabbi, Joshua O. Haberman, holds that the burden of redefining the relationship between church and synagogue must not fall solely on Christianity. Jews must examine anew the place of the Church in Jewish theology and ask how far the election and the covenant with Israel apply also to Christians. He would reinterpret the concept of election to include Christian men and women as God's elect without diffusing the uniqueness of the role of Judaism. The Jewish consciousness of election should be understood as difference, not superiority.[33]

I have encountered only one systematic attempt to formulate a contemporary Jewish document on Christianity. It is again by a US Reform rabbi (this path is unlikely to be trodden by Orthodox thinkers), Samuel Sandmel, an authority on early Christianity and Jewish attitudes to Jesus and Christianity, and author of the statement: 'I do not regard Judaism as objectively superior to Christianity nor Christianity to Judaism. Rather Judaism is mine and I consider it good and I am at home in it and I love it. That is how I want Christians to feel about their Christianity.'[34] His proposed declaration is the formulation of an individual but as the only example of its kind I cite it at length:

> The Synagogue views the Christian people as among its offspring. It acknowledges that Christian people have laudably spread the message of the Synagogue among people and in areas of the world beyond where the Synagogue had penetrated. The Christian people have adapted that message to their own character and their own ways of thinking and speaking, and they have both preserved much which is familiar to the Synagogue, and also created much which is not. Man, in his weakness, has been incapable of maintaining unbroken unity. Neither the Synagogue nor the Church has been free from division , and a by-product of such division has been irreligious hatred, bitter recrimination, and persecution, both within and without. The Synagogue laments all such manifestations within its past, and respecting the present and the future repudiates them as inauthentic manifestations of the spirit of Judaism. The Synagogue holds that its message must spread not by power or by might but only by the Spirit of God and in the love of mankind. The Synagogue is aware that Christian assemblies, lamenting and disavowing the Christian persecution of Jews, have spoken in recent times in the same vein. The Synagogue welcomes these pioneer utterances. The Synagogue cannot and does not hold innocent Christians of our day responsible, in the present or the future, for the misdeeds which may come from some.
>
> The Synagogue continues to look forward to that day when all men will become spiritually united. Since all universals are attained only through particulars, the Synagogue is committed to the perpetuation of itself against all forms of dissolution. It understands the election of Israel as imposing on it a heavier obligation to God, not as an unseemly preferment. It welcomes into its midst all those who voluntarily wish to enter. It does not seek to dissolve the institutions of its offspring nor does it cherish the abandonment by Christians of their Christian loyalties. Rather it desires that its offspring attain and maintain the spiritual heights which they often nobly expressed.
>
> The Synagogue envisages the unity of mankind in a lofty spiritual bond, enabling man both to preserve the institutions which they hold sacred and to transcend them.[35]

This statement is still a long way from what most advocates of a Jewish statement would want and it skirts basic controversial issues, but it is a start. Let me end this chapter with the words of Abraham Joshua Heschel expressing the noble concepts that have developed. He asks what is the purpose of interreligious co-operation and answers:

> It is neither to flatter nor to refute one another but to help one another; to share insight and learning, to cooperate in academic venture on the highest scholarly level, and what is even more important to search in the wilderness for wellsprings of devotion, for treasures of stillness, for the power of love and care for man. What is urgently needed are ways of helping one another in the terrible predicament of here and now by the courage to believe that the word of the Lord endures for ever as well as here and now; to cooperate in trying to bring about a resurrection of sensitivity, a revival of conscience; to keep alive the divine sparks in our souls, to nurture openness to the spirit of the Psalms, reverence for the words of the prophets, and faithfulness to the living God.[36]

Notes

1 For the first section of this chapter, see references in W. Jacob, *Christianity through Jewish Eyes*, Cincinnati, 1974.
2 Quoted in A. Altmann, *Moses Mendelssohn*, Philadelphia, 1973, p. 262.
3 *Christian – Jewish Relations*, June 1986, p. 3.
4 *Judaism*, Winter 1976, pp. 74ff.
5 *Judaism*, Summer 1978, pp. 324ff.
6 J. Isaac, *The Teaching of Contempt*, New York, 1964.
7 I. Maybaum, *The Face of God After Auschwitz*, Amsterdam, 1965, pp. 32ff.
8 *Judaism*, Summer 1967, pp. 272-3.
9 E. Fackenheim, *To Mend the World*, New York, 1982, p. 284.
10 E. Fackenheim, *The Jewish Return into History*, New York, 1978, *passim; Commentary*, August 1968, pp. 34ff.
11 I. Greenberg in *Jew and Christians after the Holocaust*, ed. A. Peck, Philadelphia, 1982, pp. 11ff.
12 U. Tal, *Patterns in the Contemporary Jewish – Christian Dialogue* (Hebrew), Jerusalem, 1969, pp 50ff.
13 *Christian – Jewish Relations*, December 1983, pp. 11ff.
14 H. Siegman in *Fifteen Years of Dialogue, 1970-1985*, Rome, forthcoming.
15 *Ibid.*
16 *Tradition*, Vo. 6 No. 2, 1964, pp. 5ff.
17 *Loc. cit.* (note 23).

18 *Judaism*, Winter 1971, p. 95.
19 *Ibid.*, p. 100.
20 *Judaism*, Summer 1966, pp. 259ff.
21 See *Modern Theologians: Christians and Jews*, ed. T. E. Bird, London 1967, pp. 180ff.
22 E. Borowitz, *How Can a Jew Speak of Faith Today?*, Philadelphia, 1969, pp. 210-211.
23 A. A. Cohen, *The Myth of the Judeo-Christian Tradition*, New York, 1971, *passim*.
24 Y. Leibowitz, *Yahadut, Am Yisrael u-Medinat Yisrael*, Jerusalem, 1975, pp. 324ff.
25 *Face to Face*, Fall-Winter 1977, p. 13.
26 *Judaism*, Winter 1971, pp. 93ff.
27 *Ecumenical Trends*, April 1986. p. 60.
28 J. Pawlikowski, *What are They Saying about Christian–Jewish Relations?*, New York, 1980, p. 87.
29 L. Boadt in *Twenty Years of Jewish-Catholic Relations*, New York, 1986, p. 101.
30 *Loc. cit.* (note 14).
31 M. Tanenbaum in *Twenty Years* (see note 29), p. 54.
32 M. Waxman in *More Stepping Stones to Jewish-Christian Relations*, ed. H. Kroner, New York, 1985, p.30.
33 *Central Conference of American Rabbis Journal*, Summer 1977.
34 S. Sandmel, *We Jews and Jesus*, New York, 1965, p. 151.
35 S. Sandmel, *We Jews and You Christians*, New York, 1967, pp. 144-6.
36 A.J. Heschel in *Disputation and Dialogue*, ed. F. E. Talmadge, New York, 1975, p. 359.

CHAPTER III

The Vatican and the Jews

Scarcely more than a century ago, in 1870, the Italian army occupied Rome which, until that time, had been under Papal rule. Only then were the city's Jews liberated from their ghetto to which they had been consigned three centuries earlier by the popes of the Counter-Reformation and condemned to live in conditions of the utmost deprivation. Had it not been for the Italian liberation, it is entirely likely that the Papacy would have kept the Jews of Rome in conditions of medieval subjection until well into the present century. In other words, despite – or perhaps because of – the winds of Enlightenment blowing in Europe, the Vatican remained locked in its ancient anti-Semitism, harbouring the traditional stereotypes and still seeing the Jews as destined for eternal punishment.

A telling episode occurred in 1904 when Theodor Herzl, father of modern Zionism, succeeded in obtaining an audience with Pope Pius X to explain to him the objectives of the new movement. According to Herzl's account, the Pope's reaction was unequivocal:

> The Jews have not recognised our Lord, therefore we cannot re-cognise the Jewish people. It is not pleasant to see the Turks in possession of our Holy Places but we have to put up with it; but we could not possibly support the Jews in the acquisition of the Holy Places. If you come to Palestine and settle your people there, we shall have churches and priests ready to baptise all of you.[1]

To the Catholic Church, then, the Jew remained accursed for his rejection of Jesus. He was not to be eliminated (or, as later terminology would say, exterminated) but was marked out in exile, degraded, until he saw the light. Down the centuries, the Church in its legislation had ensured the humiliation of the Jews and brought up generation after generation to despise them in what the French thinker Jules Isaac characterised as 'the teaching of contempt'. Thus as late as 1924 the pastoral council of the Catholic church in the Netherlands could decree: 'Parish priests must take care that Christians do not work for Jews. The faithful must take care never to need the help or support of Jews', a regulation that was annulled only in 1970![2]

Little changed in the Catholic Church's attitude to Jews up to the Second World War. In 1936, for example, the Polish Cardinal Hlond called for a strengthening of Poland's anti-Jewish legislation, already notorious for its severity. Here and there an individual would speak up against the majority and a flicker of recognition even appeared at the top. Pope Pius XI was a precursor of new attitudes in his 1937 encyclical, 'Mit brennender Sorge', which condemned racism, and in a 1938 speech he stated: 'Anti-Semitism is unacceptable. Spiritually we are all Semites.' His successor Pius XII was the controversial Pope of the war years. On the one hand, the Vatican and the Italian clergy made a great and largely successful effort to save Italian Jewry when the Germans took over the country; but on the other hand, the Pope failed to take a public stand against Hitler and Nazism, which even received support in certain Catholic circles. Papal delegates in countries where the Holocaust horror was implemented usually failed to protest, and when they did attempt to intervene it was frequently only on behalf of those Jews who had become baptised Christians – to Hitler these were still Jews but to the Church they had been saved, and therefore merited protection. The Pope himself never spoke up against the extermination of the Jews, although there is no doubt that the Vatican was well aware of what was happening. It has been suggested that a public denouncement would have had an important moral effect and the silence of the Church in the face of ultimate evil came to be widely criticised.[3]

After the war, it took time for the implications of the Holocaust to be fully realised and then haunting questions arose and challenges had to be faced. Pius XII invited Jules Isaac to an audience and heard from him that Nazi anti-Semitism was a secular radicalisation of the anti-Jewish impulses of historic Christianity. The Pope was moved to make a change in the Good Friday prayer which read: 'Let us pray for the perfidious Jews that our Lord and God will remove the veil from their hearts so that they too may acknowledge our Lord, Jesus Christ. Heed the prayers we offer for the blindness of that people that they may be delivered from their darkness.' In the late 1950s the Pope changed the prayer. Instead of 'perfidious Jews', the prayer was now merely for 'the unbelieving Jews'.

Nostra Aetate

The revolution in the attitude of the Church as a whole, was set in motion by the remarkable John XXIII, who in his brief five-year pontificate inaugurated a new era in the history of the Church. He too had been influenced by Jules Isaac as well as by his own wartime experiences as apostolic delegate in the Balkans. At the same time, pressures were beginning to build up in certain Western Catholic circles for revisions in teachings concerning Jews. When he convened the Vatican Council, John insisted that its agenda include a statement on the Jews, which he entrusted to his friend and confidant, the German Cardinal Bea, whose feelings on the subject corresponded with his own.

This began the development of the Vatican Council's Declaration on the Jews, one of the most bitterly fought-over pronouncements of the Council. At the very outset, Bea explained that its content was solely religious and its purpose spiritual. Correctly anticipating opposition from Arab Catholics, he stressed that it could in no way be considered political and therefore could not be called pro-Zionist, nor could there be any question of the Holy See recognising the State of Israel. This, however, did not still the frantic opposition of the churches in the Muslim lands and their representatives at the Council. Equally bitter hostility was encountered on theological grounds among conservative clergy, including leading and influential members of the Curia.

To them, Jews remained spiritually blind, they had turned their backs on God and were reprobate and accursed, and the church had no obligation to the Jews other than that which it had to all peoples – to confront them with the truth in Christ. The opposition elements succeeded in preventing the adoption of the document until almost the very end of the Council and then only after the introduction of certain modifications and changes. Thus in the original statement, 'May Christians never present the Jewish people as one rejected, cursed or guilty of deicide', the words 'guilty of deicide' were omitted (the Arab Catholics feeling that if the guilt of deicide was expunged, the Jews would no longer have to incur the punishment of exile and therefore there would be no objection to their returning to their land). The conservatives felt that the renunciation of deicide was a denial of the Gospel story. Care was taken to state explicitly that the authorities of the Jews and those who followed their lead pressed for the death of Christ. In another change introduced in the document, anti-Semitism was not 'condemned' but merely 'deplored'. Nowhere in the document was there any expression of contrition or repentance for the long record of Jewish suffering at the hands of the Church. There was no reference to the nature of God's covenant with the Jewish people after Jesus: it did not refer to the continuing role of the Jewish people after New Testament times, and whether they still had a mission; it did not mention the Holocaust nor, of course, the State of Israel.[4]

But the important fact was that the document – only fifteen Latin sentences – was passed and, in the end, by an overwhelming majority, as part of the Declaration on the Relation of the Church to non-Christian religions, of which it was the major component. The Declaration is known, after its opening words, as *Nostra Aetate*. Its very tone constitutes a breakthrough. For example, its stress on the spiritual bond between the Church and the Jewish people and the statement that the Church 'received the Old Testament through the people with whom God concluded the Ancient Covenant' were unprecedented. The acknowledgement of the Judaic roots of Christianity, starting with the Jewish roots of Jesus himself, opened up vistas not previously possible in

Church circles. The statement that the Jews were not rejected or accursed by God marked a turn-round in Church doctrine as was the teaching that 'what happened in the passion of Christ cannot be charged against all Jews without distinction living at that time and certainly not against the Jews living today'. Its repudiation of anti-Semitism and advocacy of mutual understanding through biblical and theological studies and fraternal dialogue were to usher in a new era in Catholic–Jewish relations.

Liberal Catholic critics, such as A. C. Ramselaar and Cornelius Rijk, noted that whenever the document discusses non-Jewish religions, such as Hinduism, Buddhism and Islam, these are described in the authentic terms of those religions themselves. Only the Jewish religion is not accorded this right and even where the Church acknowledges its truths, they lack autonomous status.[5] Similarly, as the Israeli scholar Uriel Tal pointed out, while Judaism became a partner in the dialogue, it still does not exist in its own right, but by virtue of two motifs which deprived it of autonomy: 1) the historical fact, according to the Church, that the New Testament was basically latent in the Old; and 2) the eschatological conception according to which the completion of redemption will be made possible when Judaism acknowledges that this redemption was indeed foreseen and basically latent within itself.[6]

Other statements of the Vatican Council preserved traditional viewpoints. The documents of the Dogmatic Constitution stated that the election of Israel was made by way of preparation and as a figure of that new and perfect covenant which was to be ratified in Christ, and this was the new people of God. The Dogmatic Constitution on Divine Revelation, while speaking highly and with understanding of the Old Testament, concludes that the books of the Old Testament show forth their full meaning only in the New Testament. The supersessionist implications of these documents have been carried over, as we shall see, to subsequent Vatican pronouncements.

By the time *Nostra Aetate* had been promulgated, Pope John had died and been succeeded by Pope Paul VI whose personal views were more ambivalent than those of his predecessor. On the one hand it was he who abolished the Good Friday prayer about the unbelieving Jews; but on the other hand, in a Lenten homily delivered before the Council, he referred to the Jews as a people who had fought, slandered, injured, and in the end killed Christ! He was more of a diplomat than John and was very much aware of the strength of conservatism in the Church, especially in the Vatican. In the end, it was he who was called upon to execute the far-reaching decisions of the Council which he was to accomplish with considerable tact. Under his direction, it was the spirit of *Nostra Aetate* which motivated the relationship with the Jews.

The long-term impact of the Declaration was not so much perhaps in what it actually said as in the new attitudes it initiated. A completely new vocabulary was now employed in referring to the Jews and this contributed to the creation of a fresh atmosphere conducive to mutual understanding and dialogue. At the same time, obstacles remained. An inkling of these can be gathered from Cardinal Bea's book *The Church and the Jewish People*, a commentary on the Declaration from the person most responsible for piloting it through. Writing in a positive spirit he says, for example, that deicide can only be properly imputed to those who committed the crime in the full and clear knowledge of the dual nature of Christ, and he asks whether the Sanhedrin had such knowledge, quoting St Peter's 'I know that you acted in ignorance as did your rulers'. (Acts 3: 15, 17), Jesus's 'Father forgive them for they know not what they do' (Luke 23: 24), and Paul's 'Those who live in Jerusalem and their rulers did not recognise him nor understand the utterance of the prophets' (Acts 13: 27). But also in Bea we can see certain limits in his comprehension of Jewish self-understanding. 'Evidently the Jewish people is no longer the people of God in the sense of an institution of the salvation of mankind, not because it is rejected but its function in preparing the kingdom of God finished with the advent of Christ and the founding of the Church.'[7] From then on, he explains, the nature of the 'people of God' changed and was no longer propagated by descent but by faith, nor was it confined to a single nation. No-one, he says, can take from the Jews the honour of the past in preparing the way for redemption. The Church is grounded in this people and we have God's assurance that their lack of faith will not last for ever.

We seem here to be reaching an impasse. Bea, the most outstandingly well-disposed member of the Catholic hierarchy, is in fact saying that the mission of the Jews ceased with the advent of Christ and that the Church must now wait for them eventually to accept him. But have we Jews the right to expect anything different if we in our turn respect the Catholic Church's self-definition? From ancient times, it taught that outside the Church there was no salvation, and it therefore followed that Judaism, as well as all other non-Christian religions, were, to say the least, mistaken and on the wrong track. Although the Ecumenical Council radically changed this teaching, the Church must work for – or at least anticipate – an ultimate ideal in which all men – including, and perhaps especially including, the Jews – will find their way to Christ. Meanwhile they are to be respected, even honoured, but in the knowledge that their mission was accomplished long ago. Obviously this line of thinking is unacceptable to Jews and represents a very real and basic gulf, from which there is no way out along the lines propounded, for example, by the Jew Franz Rosenzweig (see p. 52) or the Protestant Paul Van Buren (see p. 43). For this reason, many Jews today remain suspicious of Catholic dialogue. Already in 1965 the Jewish reaction to the Declaration was mixed. Some resented it, as it was widely reported that it 'absolved' the Jews of guilt for the Crucifixion, but as Jews never recognised the accusation, they saw the so-called absolution as an artificial non-issue. They also objected to other aspects that we have noted: the absence of any expression of contrition or regret for the long history of church-inspired suffering of the Jews, the non-mention of the Holocaust or the State of Israel. Others were indifferent, feeling that events had outstripped rhetorical declarations. But others welcomed it as a major turning-point, notably for the opportunities it opened up.

Under Paul VI

Pope Paul VI took a number of further steps. He extensively revised the prayer 'For the conversion of the Jews' into a prayer 'For the Jews'. He also put an end to the veneration of Simon of Trent, the boy beatified in the sixteenth century because it was believed he had been ritually murdered by Jews. (Incidentally, a similar attempt by the Catholic authorities to abolish the veneration of a three-year-old boy supposedly murdered by Jews as a blood sacrifice in the village of Rinn in the Austrian Tyrol is being resisted to this day by the villagers, as they fear that the cessation of this pilgrimage would harm them economically!)

Nostra Aetate generated a momentum among Catholics in many countries in Europe and America. The extent of the reaction depended on the degree of liberalism within the local Church and sometimes on the extent of the local Jewish presence. It was particularly strong in countries where Catholics themselves were in a minority, such as North America, Holland and Germany, but slower to develop in Catholic-dominated countries such as Poland and Spain.

Under Paul VI the new relationship became institutionalised. The first formal meeting between representatives of the Church and of World Jewry was held in Rome in 1970, the Jews being represented by the newly-constituted International Jewish Committee for Interreligious Consultations (IJCIC) which since that time has conducted dialogue on behalf of the Jewish world with roof Christian bodies – Catholic, Protestant and Orthodox. It forms the Jewish side of the Vatican Liaison Committee with the Jews which meets regularly, sometimes to discuss broad themes, sometimes to examine current developments. While the Vatican would prefer an exclusively religious dialogue, the Jews raise political issues, often related to Israel. On the Catholic side, Pope Paul VI in 1974 established a Commission for Religious Relations with Judaism which is officially described as 'attached to but independent of the Secretariat for Christian Unity. This apparently anomalous linkage springs from both historical and theological motivations. Historically, it is based on the concept that the first schism in the Church was the break with Judaism and so unity within the Church requires some form of reconciliation with the Jews. Theologically the special bond with Jews precluded the other possible connection – namely, with the Secretariat for Relations with non-Christian Religions. However, the Commission is seen as independent of the Christian Unity Secretariat so that its objective could not be misconstrued as working towards union instead of its declared goals of dialogue and reconciliation.

Still under Paul VI, the Vatican in 1974 issued a second document on the Jews in the form of 'Guidelines for the Implementation of *Nostra Aetate*'.[8] Although there was some disappointment in Jewish circles when it was issued, resulting from a number of modifications of the original draft, the 'Guidelines' went far beyond the original Declaration, giving explicit expression to the new attitudes regarding the Jews. In retrospect, it is seen as a most significant document. It laid down that Christians must strive to learn how Jews define themselves in the light of their own religious experience and must respect the Jews as they are, especially in their faith. It warned against interpreting the Old Testament and Judaism as a religion of fear, justice and legalism with no love of God and neighbour, taken to be a contribution of the New Testament. It also disputed the familiar teaching of the fossilisation of Judaism by stating that its history did not end with the destruction of Jerusalem but that it has continued to develop a rich, religious tradition. All forms of anti-Semitism were now firmly condemned, not merely deplored; the Jews of today are called 'the Jewish people' and even 'Jewish brothers'; supersessionist implications are avoided and the 'Guidelines' call on Christians 'to strive to understand the difficulties which arise for the Jewish soul – rightly imbued with an extremely high, pure notion of the divine transcendence when faced with the mystery of the incarnate word'.

Mission and witness

The impact of these fresh orientations was expressed in various ways, the most dramatic of which was the overnight abandonment of the direct Catholic mission to the Jews. For sixteen centuries, the Church Triumphant had sought by every possible method, including compulsion, to bring Jews to Christianity. Now, in the post-Holocaust world, it recognised that the time had arrived to put an end to such activity. The new approach was expressed most clearly in a 1977 paper presented by Professor Tommaso Federici at a meeting of the Catholic–Jewish Liaison Committee and with the full approbation of the Holy See.

Federici distinguished between 'witness' and 'proselytism'. 'Witness' he defined as the permanent action in which the Christian proclaims the action of God in history and tries to show how with Christ has come the true light. 'Proselytism' in some contexts has kept its original meaning of zeal for the propagation of faith but in other contexts has assumed a pejorative sense which he suggests should always be termed 'unwarranted proselytism'. This stands outside Christian witness and includes everything that forces and violates the right to be free from any constrictions in matters of religion. The Church rejects every kind of preaching and testimony that becomes any sort of constraint on the Jews, as individuals or community, that could destroy or diminish personal judgement and free will to decide. Excluded also are contempt or prejudice against Jews and Judaism as well as forms of discussion seeking to exalt Christianity by discrediting Judaism, past or present. Certainly any action seeking to change the religious faith of the Jews by the offer of any kind of advantage or using any threat or coercion is excluded. Liberty of conscience is to be guarded at every level. The attempt to create organisations of any kind to convert Jews is rejected.[9]

This remarkable statement has been recognised as setting forth Vatican policy and indeed has guided the Catholic Church in the past decade. The cessation of the Catholic mission to the Jews has been one of the most notable achievements of the Jewish–Catholic dialogue. Federici's clear distinction between witness and unwarranted proselytism provides a model which could well be studied by certain other churches.

The Vatican Council decree on the Missionary Activity of the Church saw the Church as a missionary by nature, saying 'It is God's plan that the whole body of men which makes up the human race should form one people of God and be joined in one body of Christ', whereas the Declaration on Human Freedom reflects an appreciation for religious pluralism in the whole world as a divinely given reality.[10] Even before Federici's statement, Catholic theologians were moving in a similar direction. Paul Démann distinguished between Israel and missionisable people. The Christian missionary task, he said, is to implant and give flesh to the Gospel in a soil that has been alien. Since Israel is the mother-soil out of which Christianity has grown, the concept of mission is not applicable and must be replaced by an ecumenical outlook.[11] In a similar vein Hans Küng wrote: 'The Church can never seriously take up the task of missionising the Jews. The Gospel cannot be presented to them as something alien and external. They have never been guilty of false faith. In fact before the Church existed, they believed in the one true God.'[12]

Episcopal statements

To some extent, the Vatican was moved along a more liberal path by the initiatives taken at a local level by national Catholic episcopate bodies, which went much further than the Vatican and often set the pace. They took their cue from the 'Guidelines' and made serious contributions to Catholic-Jewish understanding. In some cases, they testified to the positive encounter between Catholic and Jewish communities in their countries of origin. An outstanding example is the document published by the Brazilian bishops in 1984 (with a follow-up booklet issued in 1986 on how to teach about Jews and Judaism in Catholic schools). In it they stressed the need for Catholics to learn by what essential traits the Jews define themselves, namely by religious and ethnic elements. Judaism must not be equated with other religions because through it monotheism entered history. God Himself constituted the Hebrews as a people after making a covenant with them. The Brazilians declared that God gave the ancient land of Canaan to Abraham and the rights of the Jews to a calm political existence in their country of origin, the State of Israel, must be acknowledged – without letting this create injustice or violence for other peoples.[13] A 1980 statement by the German bishops on the Church and the Jews begins: 'He who encounters Jesus Christ encounters Judaism' and calls for changes in New Testament interpretations relating to the Jews, saying that negative New Testament statements on Jews must always be balanced with corrective New Testament statements, of which it gives examples. It lists the common ground between Christians and Jews, calling the Judaic–Christian religion 'the anti-opium for all people'.[14] A notable document issued by the French Episcopal Committee begins: 'The existence of the Jewish people and its partial ingathering in the Land of the Bible constitute increasingly for the Christian the basis of a better understanding of his own faith and a greater enlightenment for his own life'. This declaration is said to be based on a return to scriptural sources, marking a break with the attitude of an entire past. Christians have to adopt a new attitude to the Jewish people not only in the sphere of human relations but also in that of faith, which it proceeds to examine in understanding depth. It describes anti-Semitism as a heritage from the pagan world, increased in Christian times by pseudo-theological arguments. It affirms that contrary to a very ancient but contestable exegesis, it cannot be concluded from the New Testament that the Jews have been deprived of their election.[15] The Dutch bishops in 1970 affirmed that the Church must reflect on Jewish self-understanding while the Bible cannot be understood without familiarity with the Jewish awareness of God and Jewish understanding of Biblical terms. Three years later, a Belgian Catholic statement asserted: 'To insist that the Church has taken the place of the Jewish people as a salvific institution is a facile interpretation. The Church may call herself 'people of the covenant' only to the extent that she lives according to the message of Jesus. She will not be that people fully until the end of time.' This thesis negates the theological tradition that the

Church, with the coming of Jesus, displaced the Jews in God's plan.[16] In 1975 the American bishops issued an extended pastoral message 'The Church and the Synagogue'[17] and other positive documents could be cited from other countries.[18]

Under John Paul II

The general upbeat development was underlined by a number of statements coming from Catholic spokesmen, led by John Paul II, imbued with deep understanding for Judaism and the Jews. Thus the Pope, addressing representatives of the German Jewish community in Mainz in 1980 (he has made it a practice to meet with representatives of Jewish communities wherever possible on his extensive travels) spoke of 'the depth and richness of our common inheritance bringing us together in mutually trustful collaboration'. He describes Judaism as a *living* legacy that must be understood by Christians and spoke of a dialogue between today's churches and today's people of the covenant concluded with Moses.[19] This speech evoked a detailed interpretation by Archbishop John Roach, president of the National Conference of Catholic Bishops in the United States, who discerned three dimensions of dialogue in the Pope's remarks. The first flowed from the past, from our common origins and the roots of Christianity in Judaism. The Pope's remark that the Old Covenant was never retracted by God opens up the way for an entirely new relationship between the two living traditions on the basis of mutual respect for each other's essential religious claims. The second dimension is the encounter in the present between the Churches and today's people of the covenant concluded with Moses, i.e. the Pope insisted on the Church's acceptance of the continuing and permanent election of the Jewish people. This means a Christian appreciation for Judaism's own self-definition and an awareness that the Church has a very real stake in the survival and prosperity of the Jewish people. The third dimension is oriented towards the future and implies joint social action as a religious enterprise.[20]

In a further address in 1982, the Pope stressed that the two religious communities were linked at the very level of their identities. The link between the Church and the Jewish People is grounded in the design of the God of the covenant. He deplored the terrible persecutions suffered by the Jews (indeed in Australia in 1986 he was to call acts of discrimination and persecution against the Jews 'sinful') and called for Christians and Jews to hold more in-depth exchanges based on their own identities. 'Our common spiritual heritage is considerable and we can find help in understanding certain aspects of the Church's life by taking into account the faith and religious life of the Jewish people, as professed and lived now as well.' We shall be able, he said, 'to go by diverse – but in the end convergent – paths with the help of the Lord who has never ceased living with His people, to reach true brotherhood in reconciliation, respect and the full accomplishment of God's plan in history'.[21] It can be seen what advances had been made in Papal pronouncements on the Jews. In some Jewish dialogue circles the reference to 'diverse – but in the end convergent – paths' was interpreted as an indication that the Pope might be thinking along the lines indicated two generations earlier by Rosenzweig and Buber. They were to be disappointed.

Other Vatican leaders prominent in developing 'the Jewish connection' could be quoted for heartening expressions of understanding. Cardinal Martini of Milan stated in 1984:

> The Jewish people as a whole and each individual Jew considers himself as the firstborn son of the Father, called upon to praise him. According to the New Testament, the Church is the messianic people at the service of the covenant between God and man, God and mankind, God and universe. But as can be seen in both cases, there is a common service to the same project of alliance. This service constitutes a priestly ministry, a mission that can unite us without confusing us with one another until the Messiah comes'.[22]

Cardinal Etchegeray, now head of the Vatican Commission for Justice and Peace, put it this way in 1981: 'As soon as Jews and Christians begin to examine together their contrary relations throughout history, is it not possible that they will discover themselves in God's plan as two forms of the single People of God, as

Franz Rosenzweig thought?'[23] and pursuing the theme at the Rome synod of 1983 he said: 'As in the parable, neither of the two sons can gain possession of the entire inheritance, each one is for the other, without jealousy, a witness to the gratuitousness of the Father's mercy.'[24]

The Jew in Catholic religious education

The innovations in the attitudes of the Church obviously required revisions in prayers, catechisms and textbooks, still redolent of the old tradition. After the Vatican Council, many of the grosser statements were eliminated from textbooks, especially on the subject of deicide. However, according to a number of studies made by Catholics,[25] there remain cases in which the Jews are still depicted as typical examples of bad faith. They are posited as examples not to be followed, a foil contrasted with Christians and Christian beliefs. The positive aspects of Judaism are seen as culminating in Christianity while Judaism's value as a religion is described as exhausted in its contributions to the Christian heritage. Although some improvement on the 'fossilisation' view of Judaism is to be noted after the Council, the idea widely expounded is that by the time of Jesus, Judaism was merely a legalistic observance, and often no continuity is perceived between Judaism and Christianity. 'The Jews are the world's saddest people because they turned away from Jesus' is one textbook quote.[26] The Catholic experts engaged in the analysis of the textbooks stress the importance of teaching the Old Testament, the nature of Judaism and the events of Jewish history in their own right. This should be done, they say, without the traditional tag that the events of the Old Testament are to be seen as prefigurations of the New Testament events.

Most negative references in the textbooks are concerned with the rejection of Jesus and the Divine curse, the events of the Passion, and the attitude of the Pharisees. The experts point out that the problem with a Christianity which sees itself as a new Israel, a new Moses, a new covenant and a New Testament is that it leaves little, if any, room for understanding the continuation of Judaism and the relevance of the so-called 'old' Israel in the post-Biblical world. They advocate the affirmation of the value of the *whole* Bible, without making its parts antithetical; the stressing of the profound Jewishness of Jesus and his teaching; the development of the ability to use Jewish sources; the teaching of the links between the Christian and Jewish liturgies; and the emphasis on the continuity of Christianity with the earlier covenant.

Moving to later periods, there is unanimity concerning two serious gaps in Christian catechesis on the Jews: the virtual ignoring of post-Biblical Judaism and of the development of anti-Semitism, especially the Christian aspects. Because Catholic students are deprived of meaningful exposure to post-Biblical Judaism, they see Judaism as anachronistic and are unprepared for encounter with the contemporary Jew. Even in the seminaries, there are very seldom courses on post-Biblical literature and even fewer on Christian anti-Semitism. On the Holocaust there is virtual silence, and certainly no awareness of any Christian responsibility. The American scholar, Father Edward Flannery, is quoted as saying:

> The history of anti-Semitism is absent from Christian history books. Histories of the Middle Ages – and even of the Crusades – can be found in which the word 'Jew' does not appear. There are Catholic dictionaries and encyclopedias in which the term 'anti-Semitism' is not listed. The pages Jews have memorised have been torn from our history of the Christian era.[27]

Finally, Zionism and Israel are ignored, perhaps – it is suggested – because they upset the 'proof-by-punishment' theory. These experts recommend that recognition be given to these developments as part of the understanding of the Jew today and an acknowledgement of Israel's elementary right to exist. If Christians are to take seriously the directions set by the Vatican Council, they must grapple with two fundamental realities in present-day Jewish consciousness – the Holocaust and Israel.

The 1985 'Notes'

In 1985, the Vatican published its third document on Christian–Jewish relations, originally entitled 'Notes on the correct way to present the Jews and Judaism in preaching and catechesis of Catholic Church', later called, more simply, 'The Common Bond'.[28] In view of the many positive statements heard during previous years by top Vatican clerics and the realisation among Catholic educators of the need for drastic revisions in the field of teaching, Jewish expectations were high. When the document was published, Jewish reaction was mixed, with disappointment predominating. The 'Notes' contained many significant advances but at the same time restated traditional positions, which it had been hoped had been abandoned. Before its publication, the document had been examined at all levels of the Vatican and a careful analysis would seem to indicate the influence of conflicting, even contradictory, views reflecting both liberal and conservative opinions which, in turn, echo the wider controversies raging in the Church.

On the positive side, the Notes cite and affirm what is called 'the remarkable theological formula' of the Pope speaking in Mainz: 'The people of God of the Old Covenant which has never been revoked'. The incorporation of this statement in an official Vatican document constitutes an important step forward, whose full significance remains to be explored.

A further courageous statement with profound implications is the warning of the care to be taken in reading certain New Testament texts:

> It cannot be ruled out that some references hostile or less than favourable to the Jews have their historical context in conflicts between the nascent Church and the Jewish community. Certain controversies reflect Christian-Jewish relations long after the time of Jesus. To establish this is of capital importance if we wish to bring out the meaning of certain Gospel texts for the Christians today.

This recalls the recommendations of the textbook experts that the Gospels should be taught not as eye-witness accounts but as reflecting the times in which they were written, with theological speculations of the Patristic age often being retrojected into the New Testament text itself. The endorsement of this attitude, the result of modern New Testament scholarship, in a Vatican document is a tribute to the new openness of the Catholic church on these matters. The application of this recommendation could lead to the elimination of the sources of many historical frictions between Catholics and Jews and of anti-Semitic stereotypes, and it deserves to be taken up by other churches in a similar spirit.

An example of a statement wholeheartedly endorsed by Jews which admirably expresses the new relationship is this paragraph:

> Attentive to the same God who has spoken, hanging on the same word, we have to witness to one same memory and one common hope in Him who is master of history. We must also accept our responsibility to prepare the world for the coming of the Messiah by working together for social justice, respect for the rights of persons and nations, and for social and international reconciliation. To this we are driven, Jews and Christians, by the command to love our neighbour, by a common hope for the Kingdom of God and by the great heritage of the Prophets. Transmitted soon enough by catechesis, such a conception would teach young Christians in a practical way to cooperate with Jews, going beyond simple dialogue.

Also written with deep understanding are the sections covering the New Testament period – the Jewish roots of Christianity and Jews in the New Testament – which lay down clear guidelines in a manner designed to eliminate expositions likely to lead to anti-Jewish prejudices. The emphasis on the Jewishness of Jesus and the references to the Pharisees were mentioned in the first chapter (see pp. 12-14). Also welcome is the teaching that Judaism is a contemporary and not only a historical reality and the reference to the continuing fecundity of the Jews down the ages, which contradicts the former view of Judaism as ossified.

However, alongside these positive contributions, the Notes contain – in Jewish eyes – a number of negative aspects. Perhaps expectations had been buoyed unreasonably high; in that case, the Notes serve as a reminder of the boundaries of Catholic–Jewish dialogue. Alternatively, conservative influences succeeded in lowering the liberal profile, in which case an improvement could still be expected in the event of a strengthening of the liberal forces in the Catholic Church.

The basic problem is the nature of salvation. The document lays down that the Church and Judaism cannot be seen as two parallel ways of salvation and that the Church *must* witness to Christ as the redeemer for *all*. Although this is qualified by an expression of strict respect for religious liberty, its implications are clear – not only for Judaism but for all other non-Christian faiths which are allowed existential but not theological legitimation. The Church alone has the ultimate Truth and the sole path of salvation for all mankind is Jesus. This is a traditional Catholic tenet, but certain statements of the Vatican Council as well as some of the above-mentioned statements of Church leaders had pointed towards the possibility of new insights and understandings. When the Pope had said: 'We shall be able to go by diverse, but in the end convergent, paths to reach true brotherhood in reconciliation, respect and the full accomplishment of God's plan in history', he seemed to acknowledge the legitimacy of divergence and the mystery of convergence. The 'Notes' lay down that divergence must be seen as temporary, with convergence a precondition for salvation.

When I wrote along these lines in an article,[29] my interpretation was challenged by one of the most understanding and liberal of Catholic spokesmen, Eugene J. Fisher.[30] His contention is that the Notes do not imply a negative judgement regarding the salvific opportunities open to non-Christians by God's universal salvific will. To support his viewpoints he cites the Notes' statement that:

> In underlining the eschatological dimension of Christianity, we shall reach a greater awareness that the people of God of the Old and New Testament are tending toward a like end in the future: the coming or return of the Messiah – even if they start from two different points of view . . . Thus it can be said that Jews and Christians meet in a comparable hope, founded on the same promise made to Abraham.

However, I still do not feel that this answers my reading of the Notes' words: 'In virtue of her divine mission, the Church which is to be the all-embracing means of salvation in which alone the fullness of the means of salvation can be obtained must of her nature proclaim Jesus Christ to the world. Indeed we believe it is through him that we go to the Father.' I can only read this as an affirmation that the road to salvation lies through Jesus and the Church. Here, too, the deepest level of Jewish self-understanding is being negated and Jews are denied their own validity. Of course, every faith holds that it has the right way, but the issue is one of exclusivity. Judaism, so often accused of particularism, has a universal doctrine of salvation, teaching that the righteous of *all* nations of the world have their place in the world to come, i.e. salvation comes through righteous living. To quote the Israeli scholar, David Flusser:

> In the Jewish religion, the existence of Christianity (and Islam) can be understood as the fulfilment of God's promises to Abraham to make him the father of many peoples and Jews (like Moslems) are consequently less prone to occupy themselves with the theological meaning of the existence of Christianity than Christians are to speculate on the theological meaning of Judaism. It is almost impossible for them to believe that one who does not accept the Christian faith can be saved.[31]

In other words, it may be said that on the subject of salvation, Judaism's pluralism and universalism can be contrasted with Christianity's traditional exclusiveness and particularism. The Church insists on faith in Jesus as essential for full salvation and unless it is prepared to interpret this for other faiths in terms of mystery and eschatology, a note of triumphalism will be inevitable. This would appear to conflict with the Notes' own statement that a fundamental condition of dialogue is the respect for the essential traits by which the Jews define themselves in the light of their own religious experience. Moreover, running counter to the attitude to mission authoritatively propounded by Federici, the Notes imply a conversionist hope to be interpreted by every Catholic implicitly, if not explicitly, leaving Jews uncomfortable and uncertain of the true motives of the dialogue partner. Would that the document had followed the sentiments expressed by Eugene Fisher: 'The point to be remembered is not who is "most dear" to God. The point is rather what God has called us both, Jews and Christians, to do in and for the world. The issue is the building of God's Kingdom, not what place either of us feel we can claim within that Kingdom.'[32]

Linked to the concept of salvation is the validity of the election. In warning against anti-Semitism, the Notes say that the faithful should learn to appreciate and love the Jews who remain a chosen people. But, it adds, they have been chosen – to prepare the way for the coming of Christ. The definitive meaning of the election of Israel only becomes clear in the light of the complete fulfilment. Fisher finds this statement as saying nothing more than that Israel's election is a witness to and finds its ultimate destiny in God's Kingdom.[33] However, Allan R. Brockway, secretary of the World Council of Churches' Consultation on the Church and the Jewish People, wrote:

> What immediately comes to mind upon reading these words is the stance taken by the late 19th and early 20th century missions to the Jews, the archival records of which reveal a deep and profound love of the Jewish people for the very reasons adduced in the 'Common Bond'. It was out of this love that the missionaries felt it their duty to declare 'The Messiah for whom you wait has come in Jesus Christ.' Those same missionaries, moreover, evidenced an intense hatred of anti-Semitism which they decried on the identical theological basis expressed in the 'Common Bond'.[34]

We are touching on one of the document's basic ambiguities. Its initial premise is 'The people of the God of the Old Covenant which has never been revoked', which would appear to affirm the existence of two covenants, valid side by side. But what is not spelled out is the status of the first covenant after the coming of Christ. Is it still valid in its totality? Do the Jews retain an independent existence within their own view of the covenant or do they remain here solely to somehow give potential witness to Christianity and to the Parousia? Is this their sole role? In the words of the Israeli Catholic theologian, Marcel Dubois:

> In our day many Christians as well as Jews have pondered whether there is one Covenant or two between God and His people. In other words, do there exist two peoples of God, spiritually linked,

or one people of God composed of both Jews and Christians together whose mission is to proclaim the sacred name of the One God? The question is unanswerable. God alone knows the answer.[35]

On the relations between the Hebrew Bible and the New Testament, the Notes state that the Hebrew scriptures have permanent value – for Christian faith expression. There is no hint that its proclamation of monotheism, the glory of the Psalms and the social and ethical message of the Prophets have a permanent value in their own rights and that this might be a great universal document for all mankind. Instead there is an endorsement of typology, i.e. that the Old Testament is not to be read for itself but as a forecast and prefiguration of the New Testament. Following the typological approach, Jews lose their intrinsic value and do not stand on their own, becoming mere models or prototypes. Jesus is the point of reference for the Old Testament, which, similarly, does not stand on its own. The Exodus is cited as an experience of salvation and liberation that is not complete in itself; liberation is only accomplished in Christ and realised in the Church sacraments. The Church and Christians are to read the Old Testament in the light of the dead and risen Christ. As Brockway says, contemporary theological understandings of Christian faith have been made to lie on the typological procrustean bed and the supersessionist assumptions of this exegetical tool win out in the end.[36] For Jews, the use of typology has constituted an obstacle throughout the history of the church and its reaffirmation as legitimate exegesis is disquieting. The Vatican's leading ideologist, Cardinal Ratzinger, has stated in a recent book: 'We must again have the courage to say clearly that the Bible taken as a whole is Catholic'.[37] (I am reminded of a memoir of a Catholic boyhood in Dublin early in the century in which the writer says: 'We were taught to regard the Old Testament as a Protestant document, having no bearing on our faith.'[38]) All this is of course unacceptable to Jews for whom the Old Testament is neither Catholic nor Protestant, which is not in fact an 'Old' Testament, and whose Jewishness is axiomatic. To give an idea of what might have been said and welcomed, let me quote from a remarkable document which was prepared for the Holy See's Office for Relations with Judaism by a special commission in December 1969 but unfortunately not accepted. The text eventually found its way into print [39] and I cite a paragraph: 'The Old Testament should not be understood exclusively in reference to the New nor reduced to an allegorical significance as is so often done in Christian liturgy.' Here is a statement made by Catholic experts expressing the direction in which Jews would have hoped to see the subject developed. Unfortunately the opposite occurred.

In dealing with the death of Jesus, the Vatican Notes continue the line proposed in *Nostra Aetate* and treat the subject with understanding and discernment. However, they fall into a trap, albeit out of the best of intentions. To move away from the Church's historical construction of laying the blame for Jesus's death on all Jews then living and who have lived subsequently, it says 'there is no putting the Jews who knew Jesus and who did not believe in him on the same plane with Jews who came after him or those of today'. To which, I would say 'Why not?' Continuity is absolutely fundamental to Jewish self-conception and the Jews of today would not wish to be seen on a different plane from their ancestors in the time of Jesus. Indeed those very Jews played a critical role in moulding the subsequent character of Judaism: the basis of rabbinic Judaism, the Mishnah, was being laid and the strength of the Pharisaic tradition enabled Judaism to withstand the loss of the Temple, sovereignty and independence. Their non-acceptance of Jesus has been endorsed by every succeeding generation. The problem for the Church is that having created the deicide myth and now recognising its dangers, it cannot see how to destroy it. Instead it aims at mitigation which only involves it in further historical distortions.

The last section of the Notes, subtitled 'Judaism and Christianity in History' again contains many helpful sections. However, the continuing omission of any specific reference to the Christian record of anti-Semitism (left to be inferred from the statement that the 'balance of relations between Jews and Christians over 2,000 years has been negative') is a regrettable lacuna. One Jewish reaction has said that anti-Semitism is a Christian creation and a Christian responsibility (whatever secondary causes were involved) and none of the Vatican documents confronts the Church's role, lumping it together with other forms of intolerance.[40] On the vital subject of the Holocaust, the document is almost offhand, saying merely that 'Catechesis should help in understanding the meaning for the Jews of the extermination during the years 1939-45 and its consequences.' That is all said about this traumatic event which has seared every Jewish soul and which underlies all that Jews have said or done over the past forty years, as well as underlying the entire Christian–Jewish dialogue. Unfortunate, too, is the restriction of the significance of the Holocaust to its 'meaning for the Jews', with no indication of its meaning for the Church and Christendom or of its universal implications. The Notes were the only one of the three Vatican documents on the Jews and Judaism on which Jewish circles were not consulted prior to publication. When Jewish reactions began to be expressed after publication, Vatican circles realised that they had not related adequately to the subject of the Holocaust and sought to meet the Jewish objections in their subsequent clarifications. However, a Vatican overview of this subject is still forthcoming.

In sum, for all its positive statements and subsequent clarifications by Catholic spokesmen, key sections of the document came to Jews as a disappointment because it failed to meet as completely as had been hoped the declared need to conduct the dialogue on the basis of the mutual recognition of the other's self-definition. It also fails to answer the recommendations of the Catholic experts to teach just who are the Jewish people today. In theological dialogue, the goal is not agreement but understanding, and while progress has been made, the problems indicated show the need for further elucidation.

The Pope in the synagogue

The problems were only underlined by a surprising series of statements by the Pope during the months after the Notes were issued. In October 1985, he received the Jewish–Catholic Liaison Committee gathered in Rome to celebrate the twentieth anniversary of *Nostra Aetate* and to discuss the state of Catholic-Jewish relations. The Pope assured them that *Nostra Aetate* remained an irrevocable pronouncement binding on the Church for the future. However, about the same time, the Pope in a general audience spoke of the Jews as having killed Christ.[41] Jews were horrified at this evidence of deeply-rooted prejudice, the eradication of which was supposed to have been the main achievement of *Nostra Aetate*.

Concern was heightened by a series of three Lenten sermons delivered by the Pope in March 1986. Traditional displacement theology seemed to be reaffirmed when he stated:

> Because of the many transgressions of the Covenant, God promises His chosen people a new covenant, ratified with the blood of His own son, Jesus, on the Cross. The Church, expression of the New Covenant, represents the continuity of Israel, which had wandered in search of salvation. It is the new Israel; it presupposes the old and goes beyond it, to the extent that it has the necessary strength to live not through obedience to the ancient laws, that gave knowledge of God but not His salvation, but through faith in Jesus.[42]

All three speeches were in a similar vein. Not only were Jews alarmed at these homilies but also liberal Catholic theologians, who saw in them the turning-back of the clock to a pre-Vatican Council mentality. Jewish bodies were considering an appropriately critical riposte when the announcement came that the Pope would visit the synagogue in Rome – the first visit of a Pope to a synagogue. Although by the Pope's own statement, this move had been contemplated for some time, the actual timing may have been connected with the growing malaise in Jewish circles over the effect his recent remarks could have on the dialogue. The fact that the Pope had been making seemingly contradictory statements on different occasions seemed evidence of the continuing conflict in the Vatican and Catholic hierarchy between conservative and liberal elements.

The visit by the Pope to the synagogue in Rome in April 1986 and the contents of his address[43] served to give renewed momentum to the dialogue. The speech carefully identified with progressive views, and by implication the Pope disassociated himself from the conservatives. Statements such as 'each of our religions wishes to be respected and recognised in its own identity' and 'The Lord will judge each one according to his own works, Jews and Christians alike' may have been designed to counter some of the Jewish objections to the Notes and homilies, and to acknowledge that Jewish identity had not been appropriated or substituted by Christianity. Similarly the graphic reference to Judaism as 'our elder brother' and to Jews as 'irrevocably the beloved of God' pointed in the same direction, while the statement that 'faith cannot be the object of exterior pressure' echoed Federici's denunciation of 'unwarranted proselytism'. The main disappointment among Jewish listeners was the absence of even a word concerning the State of Israel. The expectations of some Jews that the Pope would take this opportunity to make some dramatic gesture on the subject was unrealistic, but a reaffirmation of his own statement made in 1984 acknowledging the right of the Jews in Israel to security and tranquillity (see p. 118) would have been in place. But without doubt the overall thrust and effect of the speech were decidedly positive contributions to the Catholic-Jewish relationship, and its extensive media coverage ensured that the message of a new interfaith era was brought to much more extensive strata of the Catholic world than previously had been the case. It is to be hoped that the momentum attained is irreversible, but Jewish misgivings must be further dispelled by corroboration and affirmation of the message of the synagogue visit and speech through future statements and actions. At the 1985 meeting of the Catholic-Jewish Liaison Committee, held in the Vatican, a programme was proposed which included the dissemination and explanation of the achievements of the past two decades to the two communities; the overcoming of residues of indifference, resistance and suspicion; joint action in combating religious extremism and fanaticism; common action for justice and peace; and a joint study of the historical events and theological implications of the Holocaust.[44]

Looking back in perspective, the changes that have occurred within a mere two decades have been impressive. We have noted an assymetry between Christian and Jewish approaches to their relationship, but another assymetry emerges in the intra-Christian world. Churches have been proposing new theologies of Judaism and differences have opened up. Not all churches would go as far as the Catholic Church in describing Judaism as central to the interpretation of Christianity but others might be developing a more liberal doctrine of salvation. Catholic-Protestant dialogue has concentrated on other issues, not on comparisons of attitudes to Jews and Judaism, while neither Catholics nor Protestants could today accept the obscurantism of the Orthodox Churches on this subject. An aspect suggested by Pawlikowski is that the originality of the new thinking on the Jews might imply the breaking of parameters also in Catholic relationships with other non-Christian religions, and will help the Church relate to those faiths too with a new theological voice.[45]

Uriel Tal has related the hopeful developments in the Catholic-Jewish rapprochement of the post-war world to the Catholic Church's renewed confrontation with the realm of earthliness. This has introduced a common denominator with Judaism, with the Halacha, and consequently with the Jewish way of life. Basing himself on documents of the Vatican Council he discerns a renewed affirmation of the theological relevance of the world of creation, of life and survival, of existence and being, which he feels can render the traditional preoccupation of the Torah and of Judaism with the realm of earthliness more understandable to Christians.[46]

Notes

1 *The Complete Diaries of Theodore Herzl*, ed. R. Patai, New York, 1960, IV, pp. 1601ff.
2 L. Swidler in *Judaism*, Summer 1978, p. 299.
3 See, for example, S. Friedländer, *Pius XII and the Third Reich*, London, 1966; J. F. Morley, *Vatican Diplomacy and the Jews During the Holocaust*, New York, 1980; *The Storm over the Deputy*, ed. E. Bentley, New York, 1964.
4 See A. Gilbert, *The Vatican Council and the Jews*, New York, 1968, *passim*. For the text of *Nostra Aetate*, see pp. 143-4.
5 *Christians in Israel* Vol. 1X No. 1, 1966.
6 Uriel Tal, *Patterns in the Contemporary Jewish-Christian Dialogue* (Hebrew), Jerusalem, 1969.

7 A. Bea, *The Church and the Jewish People*, New York, 1966, p. 96.
8 For full text, see pp. 144-9.
9 *More Stepping Stones to Jewish–Christian Relations*, ed. H. Croner, New York, 1985, pp. 37ff.
10 *Christian Mission – Jewish Mission*, ed. M. A. Cohen and H. Croner, New York, 1982, p. 30.
11 E. Fleischner, *Judaism in German Christian Theology*, Metuchen, N.J., 1975, p. 89.
12 H. Küng, *The Church*, New York, 1967, p. 142.
13 *More Stepping Stones* (see note 9), pp. 151ff.
14 *Ibid*, pp. 124ff.
15 *Les Eglises devant le Judaïsme*, ed. M. T. Hoch and B. Dupuy, Paris, 1980, pp. 171ff.
16 *Stepping Stones to Further Jewish-Christian Relations*, ed. H. Croner, New York, 1977, p. 54.
17 *Ibid.*, pp. 29ff.
18 *Stepping Stones* (see note 16) and *More Stepping Stones* (see note 9), *passim*.
29 *Osservatore Romano* (English edition), 9 December 1980.
20 *Twenty Years of Jewish–Catholic Relations* ed. E. J. Fisher, A. J. Rudin and M. H. Tanenbaum, New York, 1986, pp. 218ff.
21 *Ibid.*, pp. 215ff.
22 *Christian–Jewish Relations*, Vol. XVII No. 4 (December 1984), p. 9.
23 *Ibid.*, Vol. 14 No. 3 (September 1981), p. 6.
24 *Ibid.*, Vol. 16 No. 4 (December 1983), p. 23.
25 J. T. Pawlikowski, *Catechetics and Prejudice*, New York, 1973, which is largely based on a study of Catholic textbooks in the US published shortly before the Vatican Council; C. H. Bishop, *How Catholics Look At Jews*, New York, 1974, an examination of Italian, Spanish and French teaching materials that appeared up to the mid-1960s; and E. Fisher, *Seminary Education and Christian– Jewish Relations*, Washington, 1983.
26 Pawlikowski, *op. cit.* (note 25), p. 79.
27 *Ibid.*, p. 44.
28 For full text, see p. 000.
29 *Midstream*, June/July 1986, pp. 11ff.
30 *Ibid.*, January 1987, pp. 61-2.
31 *Contemporary Jewish Religious Thought*, ed. A. A. Cohen and P. Mendes-Flohr, New York, 1987, pp. 61ff.
32 E. Fisher, *op. cit.* (note 25), p. 2.
33 E. Fisher, *op. cit.* (note 30).
34 A. R. Brockway, 'Reflections on Common Bond' (privately circulated).
35 *Face to Face*, Fall 1985, p. 31.
36 Brockway, *op. cit.* (note 34).
37 *The Tablet*, 7 September 1985, editorial.
38 C. S. Andrews, *Dublin Made Me*, Dublin, 1979, p. 120.
39 M. B. McGarry, *Christology after Auschwitz*, New York, 1977, pp. 21ff.
40 *Christian–Jewish Relations*, Vol. 19 No.1 (March 1986) p. 61.
41 *Osservatore Romano* (weekly English edition), 28 October 1985, p. 2.
42 *Ibid.*, 3 March 1986, p. 5; 10 March 1986, pp. 2, 11.

43 *Juifs et Chrétiens 'pour une entente nouvelle'*, ed. J. Halpérin and B. Dupuy, Paris, 1986.
44 *Christian-Jewish Relations*, Vol. 18 No.4, December, 1985, p. 6.
45 *Ecumenical Trends*, April 1986, p. 66.
46 U. Tal in *Christians and Jews*, ed. H. Küng and W. Hasper, New York, 1975, pp. 80-7.

CHAPTER IV

Israel in the dialogue

Hans Küng has commented that every religion has its neuralgic, non-negotiable points. 'For Christianity, it is the Son of God; for Islam it is the Word of God; and for Judaism it is the Land of God.'[1] While this statement suffers from the general vulnerability of aphorisms (the Word of God is no less central to Judaism than to Islam, for example), it also contains insight.

As far as the land of God is concerned, it is true that Judaism, Christianity and Islam all ascribe holiness to the same territorial region, but distinctions should be drawn. For the Muslims, the holiness applies to the two great mosques in Jerusalem and the surrounding area, the Haram al-Sharif, and at the utmost to the city of Jerusalem (in Arabic, *al-Quds*, 'The Holy One'). The rest of the land is of no special significance and indeed under Muslim rule was often merely a province of Syria. For Christians, the Land possesses a holiness, *Terra Santa*, but in fact Christian interest has been confined to those places linked to the New Testament story. It has concentrated on the Holy Places rather than the Holy Land, and ignored parts of the country, such as most of the coastal area or the Negev, not associated with Jesus and his followers. Moreover, from a very early period there was a trend in Christianity which minimised the significance of the Holy Land on the grounds that as a result of the Incarnation every place is as holy as the other. But for Jews the whole Land within its God-promised borders – variably defined already in the Bible – is sanctified. Jerusalem, the Holy City, may have a special degree of holiness, and within Jerusalem the Temple Mount enjoys the supreme sanctity, but this does not detract from the holiness of the entire Land. When a Jew died in the Diaspora he was buried with a sack of earth from the Holy Land – from any part of it – while Jews have been happy to fulfil their divine link by settling in Ascalon and Jaffa as in Hebron and Jerusalem.

This century, Christianity has had to face the issue of whether or not it can find a place in its theology for the return of the Jewish people to the Promised Land. In traditional Christian teaching, the Jews forfeited their central role in God's providence with the birth of Christianity. They had become an anachronism and the belief in the invalidation of the Old Covenant included the Jewish claim, on religious grounds, to the Land of Israel. It should be noted that the ideology of the Church Fathers that Jews have to pay for the rejection of Jesus by dispersion and continuous suffering was never a binding dogma in Christianity.[2] Nevertheless, it has been said, the relationship of covenant to Land and of the Jews to Israel is as much outside the Christian experience as the centrality of Jesus in the mystery of the triune God is outside the Jewish experience.[3] To Jews, Israel is central to their Judaism, essential to their faithfulness to the Torah; to Christians it appears peripheral and its introduction into dialogue often makes them uncomfortable. Some still today even see it as an illegitimate injection of politics. One consequence has been the determination, expressed in documents from churches of many denominations, to balance any favourable reference to the Jewish return to the land of Israel with an 'evenhanded' reference to Arab Palestinian rights, which in turn has been denounced as a distortion and the introduction of politicisation into a religious issue.[4]

Christian reaction has, in fact, been sharply divided. In the Catholic Church, the attitude to Zionism was hostile for both theological and political reasons. Theologically, the return of the Jews to the Land of Israel and the possibility of the establishment of a Jewish State contradicted long-established convictions. As mentioned earlier (p. 75), the anti-Zionist tone had already been set in 1904 by Pope Pius X in his remarks to Theodor Herzl.

Politically, the events of the First World War and its aftermath seemed to the Vatican to present the opportunity to re-establish a measure of influence in the Holy Land which had been unattainable during the long centuries of Muslim rule. Indeed, already in 1914 the British Foreign Secretary, Sir Edward Grey, contemplated a post-war neutral Palestine supervised by the European Allied Powers, the United States and the Vatican.[5] These hopes were bitterly disappointed when in 1917 effective government fell into the exclusive hands of the Protestant British, who had moreover made a commitment to the establishment of a Jewish National Home. When in December 1917 the bells of the churches of Rome pealed out to celebrate the liberation of the Holy City from the infidel, only the bells of St. Peter's remained silent.[6] The Vatican saw no cause for rejoicing at the prospect of Protestant rule or of the Jewish return. 'Should we turn even a small part of our hearts from the Turks to the Zionists?' asked the Vatican Secretary of State, while the Pope, Benedict XV, said: 'It will be greatly painful for me and for Christendom if non-believers enjoy better conditions than we do in Palestine and if the Holy Places will be handed to non-Christians. Zionist rule would be an affront to the Christian conscience.'[7] The Vatican schemed consistently to have the Mandate entrusted to a Catholic power or, failing that, towards an arrangement whereby the Holy Places would be placed under Catholic control, ignoring similar claims by other Churches. The French worked with the Vatican for the granting of the Mandate to Catholic Belgium, which would leave France as the dominant influence. The Vatican, stoutly supported by the Latin Patriarch of Jerusalem, consistently opposed any special privileges being granted to the Jews in the Holy Land, fearing that Zionist immigration would put an end to the Christian character of the country.[8]

The Holy Places continued to provide a constant source of friction. The Vatican had an elastic concept of these sites. To the Jews and Protestants, they consisted of a limited number of buildings with their grounds, long defined in the Ottoman documents, known as the Status Quo. Already in 1895 Theodor Herzl in his *Judenstaat*, the founding document of the modern Zionist movement, had advocated extra-territorial status for these places. But to the Vatican, the Holy Sites covered extensive areas – all of Jerusalem, Bethlehem, Nazareth, Tiberias, Jericho and even

Mount Carmel, which was associated with the Virgin Mary (the Vatican protested against a planned cable car route to the summit of Mount Carmel, which offended its susceptibilities). The Vatican wanted, as far as possible, to keep the Holy Land as a museum and objected, for example to using the Sea of Galilee for pleasure purposes. In the end, the Vatican was frustrated on all counts but never forgot its political ambitions, which came to the surface again in 1948.

The Protestants were free of the Catholics' theological fetters on the subject and, in their fragmentation, evolved a broad spectrum of attitudes towards Zionism. There were those who accepted the traditional teaching of discontinuity and maintained that the Jew no longer had any claims on the Land. Some of these were prepared to consider Zionism in terms of contemporary political merit but insisted that it not be backed by historical and religious considerations.

However, Protestantism also bred the opposite reaction of enthusiastic endorsement for the Jewish return to the Holy Land. Occasionally this was motivated by pure humanitarian considerations and a literal devotion to the word of the Bible, but more often the considerations were eschatological. The return of the People of Israel to the Land of Israel was seen as an essential precondition to the Parousia, at which time, it was assumed, the Jews would see the light and save themselves and the rest of mankind through their acceptance of Jesus. Thus Lord Shaftesley, the nineteenth-century British philanthropist, believed that the Jews would be recalled to their ancient rule as agents of the Christian Millennium.[9] The predeliction towards a pro-Zionist orientation in Protestant circles was primarily moulded by the impact of the Old Testament (a factor, for all practical purposes, absent from the world of the ordinary Catholic). The literal reading of the Old Testament had a strong influence in Britain[10] and although the Balfour Declaration was a purely political document, many of the key personalities involved, such as Lloyd George and Balfour, were deeply affected by their devotion to the word of the Bible.

The establishment of the State of Israel

The establishment of the State of Israel in 1948 intensified the theological dilemma of those Christian elements which had seen the Jewish exile as punishment. The vibrancy of the new Jewish state challenged the concept of Judaism as a dead and arid fossil, a burden to its people until they would see the light and accept Jesus.

The Vatican reacted with silence to the theological implications. In the aftermath of the Holocaust – with the Church's own ambivalent attitude during the war and its failure to speak out openly against the extermination of the Jews – it was prudent to remain quiet when the State was proclaimed, largely under the impact of the tragic plight of the Holocaust survivors. The United Nations decision of November 1947 on the partition of Palestine did reawaken hope in the Vatican for an extension of its influence in the Holy Land, especially as the original plan did not assign Jerusalem to either the Jews or the Arabs but left it under international control. For the next two years, the Vatican lobbied vigorously for the internationalisation of Jerusalem, hoping thereby to get its own foot in the door. *L'Osservatore Romano* (28 May 1948) emphasised that to place Christianity on a par with Muslims and Zionists in its bonds with the Holy Land was a sign of moral distance and showed a contempt for reality, while *La Civiltà Cattolica* insisted that the Catholic people's (not even the Christians') interests and rights were higher and preceded historically those of any other group of nations. The official attitude was expressed by Pope Pius XII in an encyclical of October 1948, advocating the status of a *corpus separatum* for Jerusalem.[11] The Holy See's campaign was frustrated by the emergence of facts: Israel made the New City of Jerusalem its capital and Jordan was equally firm in opposing any form of non-Muslim control for the Old City, where most of the Holy Places, which it controlled, were situated. The struggle lasted for a couple of years, after which the Vatican had to accept the new situation and put the subject on a back-burner, not even to be raised when Pope Paul VI visited the Holy Land in 1964. He spent a couple of days in Jordanian

Palestine and one day in Israel where he succeeded in never once uttering the word 'Israel', and on his departure sent a message of thanks for the hospitality he had received, addressed merely to 'President Shazar, Tel Aviv'. Any mention of Israel was studiously avoided throughout the Vatican Council except for Cardinal Bea's assurance that the document on the Jews should in no way be interpreted as any form of recognition of the State of Israel.

Protestant statements on the foundation of the State of Israel were initially mealy-mouthed. The World Council of Churches, at its first Assembly in 1948, noted that the establishment of the State added a political dimension to the Christian approach to the Jews which threatened to complicate anti-Semitism with political fears and enmities.[12] It failed to mention any other aspect or to refer to the problems of the refugees and Holocaust survivors then exercising the conscience of mankind.

By 1956, the World Council of Churches had advanced to a position of ambivalence. A study group summarised its stance on the revived nationalism of the Jewish people and the existence of the State of Israel as follows:

> We cannot say a plain *yes* to the forces of nationalism, for that would be to endorse forces of corporate selfishness and antagonism with all the suffering they cause. On the other hand we cannot say a plain *no*, because the Church does not stand for a vague cosmopolitanism. The answer lies between the *yes* and the *no*... To the State of Israel we cannot say an absolute *no*, for we must all sympathise with the sufferings of the Jewish people and rejoice whenever by God's grace they are delivered from them. Yet we cannot say an absolute *yes*, for the setting up of the State of Israel while it has relieved the sufferings of many Jews, has involved great suffering to many Arabs who have lost their land and their homes. Moreover, while we understand the desire of many Jews to have a country of their own, we believe it is their calling to live as the people of God, and not to become merely a nation like others.[13]

By 1968, the World Council of Churches' Faith and Order Commission spoke of the State as 'an event of tremendous importance for the vast majority of Jews, giving them a new feeling of assurance', qualifying this by adding that it had brought suffering and injustice to the Arab people.[14] In 1974, the Consultation on

Biblical Interpretation and the Middle East set out the contrasting theological positions so as to cater for the differing views within the World Council. It mentions those who hold that the Old Testament has no specific bearing on the Middle East today, and the view that one cannot speak of a theological or biblical relation between the modern State of Israel and the ancient state of Israel or of any connection between the election of the people of Israel in the Old Testament and the Jewish community in the world today. It then quotes the opposing view that God's promises are irrevocable and that there *is* a theological foundation for a national self-expression on the part of the Jewish people in the Land. 'Far from being nullified or transmuted by the Christ event, these promises and events are seen as confirming the faithfulness of God.'[15]

In 1983, the Unit for Dialogue with People of Living Faiths and Ideologies of the World Council of Churches issued its 'Ecumenical Considerations on Jewish-Christian Dialogue'[16] Its draft section on Israel was toned down on demands of member churches, especially from the Middle East. Omitted, for example, was the original statement: 'Of particular significance is the understanding of the indissoluble bond between the Land of Israel and the Jewish people. . . The need for the State of Israel to exist in security and peace is fundamental to Jewish consciousness and therefore is of paramount importance to any dialogue with Jews.' This proved unacceptable, as did the statement that, while the Land had special significance for Muslims and Christians, it was of an essential nature for Jews; this was changed for the statement that the Land cannot be deemed more essential for one group than another. In its final form, the document notes that there was no time in which the memory of the Land of Israel and Zion was not central in the worship and hope of the Jewish people. 'Next year in Jerusalem' was always part of the Jewish worship in the Diaspora, it notes, adding that the continued presence of Jews in the Land and Jerusalem was always more than just one place of residence among all the others. The State is for Jews part of the long search for that survival which has always been central to Judaism through the ages. It goes on to say that now the quest for statehood by Palestinians also calls for full attention. As it was felt that this document would still prove too controversial to be approved at the highest echelon, it was not submitted to the WCC Assembly but was issued at a lower level.

While the General Secretary of the World Council did reject the notorious United Nations resolution of 1975 identifying Zionism with racism, the WCC Assembly in that year refused to support him and took a political line strongly critical of Israel. Its next Assembly, in 1983, adopted a Middle East resolution condemning Israel on many issues and expressing support for the Palestine Liberation Organisation. It even charged that some Christians allow their guilt for the Holocaust to 'corrupt their views of the conflict in the Middle East' in ways that entice them into 'uncritical support' of Israeli policies,[17] a statement that Jews found deeply offensive. The World Council of Churches is deeply involved with the Third World and this connection dictates its politics, including its identification with the Palestinian Arab cause. The Middle East Council of Churches, whose membership is largely Arab, is an influential element in the World Council, while the presence of representatives of the Russian Church injects another potential anti-Israel force. Departments of the World Council of Churches have issued publications based on a hostile attitude towards Israel and in the dialogue between Jews and the World Council attitudes towards Israel remain a frequent source of friction.

The World Council – like the Vatican – has also attempted to develop a Christian–Muslim dialogue and inevitably the Muslims have placed the issue of Israel high on the agenda. This dialogue is an uphill enterprise by virtue of the nature of Islam, compounded by the contemporary resurgence of zealous fundamentalism, which threatens religious pluralism in a growing number of Muslim lands. Few of these countries are open to dialogue and the most willing Muslim participants are those in the Western world. It has been noted that Muslims often enter the dialogue in order to influence their Christian partners to condemn Israel's policies, and even its existence.[18] The 1965 Vatican *Nostra Aetate* declaration not only expressed Catholic attitudes concerning Jews but also contained an overture to Islam –

although Muslim reaction was not to welcome this opening but to attack the Jewish aspects. Since then the Vatican has attempted to develop that dialogue but with only limited success. The World Council of Churches, for its part, has chosen as its dialogue partner the World Muslim Congress, whose headquarters are in Pakistan and which has adopted the most extreme anti-Semitism and anti-Zionism in its public postures. Its official position states that the 'Zionist scourge aims at controlling the world and, if that is not possible, at annihilating the entire human race.'[19] Its President told a United Nations Seminar that 'the Talmud says that if a Jew does not drink every year the blood of a non-Jewish man, he will be damned for eternity' and claimed that 'the whole world is the property of Israel and that the wealth, blood and souls of non-Israelis belong to them'.[20] As some of the same individuals in the World Council are talking to these people and to Jewish dialogue partners, their credibility is weakened.

Several of the individual mainline Protestant Churches have issued statements concerning the State of Israel. These embody a variety of viewpoints, ranging from warm identification to cold approval combined with strong reservations and sharp criticisms. One of the earliest was a declaration on 'Israel and the Church' promulgated in 1969 by the Synod of the Netherlands Reformed Church.[21] This suggests that for the Jews the material Land of Israel is concrete evidence of the realisation of prophecy and its essential message is that earthly reality is inseparable from religious truths. The lesson is that the bond between the Land of Israel and the People of Israel is not natural, but supernatural, based on the promise to Abraham. As the patriarchs were also the Christian patriarchs, the renewed bond has biblical and prophetic significance for the Christian as well. It also means that for the Jew the renewed bond will be different from that between any other people and land, and theological necessity requires it to assume a universalist form. In Uriel Tal's analysis the effect of this demand makes the Jewish right to their land conditional, not on authentic Jewish criteria, but on universal standards – derived by Christian interpretations. Admitting that Christian nations have not succeeded in carrying out this prophetic universalism in their own states, they now expect the People of Israel to execute Biblical morality. This viewpoint has been echoed in Liberal Christian thought, Protestant and Catholic.

The Dutch Reformed Church issued another document in 1970 entitled 'Israel: People, Land and State'.[22] This contains an admixture of the approving and the critical. After stating that the enforced separation of people and land had been abnormal, it goes on to make the assertion that this cannot be said of the city of Jerusalem or of the kingship or of the independent state, which were not inherent in Israel's election, while the advent of the kingdom of God depends on the Jews accepting Jesus. The cult and the kingship which were connected with Jerusalem are fulfilled in Jesus Christ. 'We cannot imply that the people may never again be expelled from its land', it says. 'God's promise is people-land, not people-state.' But, it concludes, 'as of now only a State safeguards the existence of the people and offers them a chance to be truly themselves'.

This last phrase – 'to be truly themselves' – is the central issue for Jews. The role of Israel and Jerusalem in Jewish self-definition is crucial and the recognition of this fact is what Jews are asking from Christians today. Moments of truth came in 1967 and 1973 when Israel appeared to be in mortal danger. Jews throughout the world were shaken to the depths of their souls and sought some sort of expression of recognition of the need for the continuing existence of the State from Christians, especially from those with whom they were by then engaged in dialogue. With very few exceptions, the Christians remained silent and evasive. The main Churches refused to speak out, presumably out of political considerations of their commitments in the Muslim world. But for Jews the existence of Israel is not only a political but a religious issue and the refusal of the Churches to recognise this at the moment of testing was a severe setback to the very principle of dialogue. However it did have the salutary effect of giving the subject of Zionism and Israel more prominence in subsequent Christian–Jewish encounters, with the Jewish partners determined to make Christians understand how indispensable Israel was to them.

The Evangelicals

The Restoration Movement, originating mainly with pietistic Protestants in sixteenth-century England, aimed at promoting the return of the Jews to the Holy Land. It was based on a millenarian interpretation of the Bible according to which Jesus would return to earth for a thousand-year rule and that either before or after this Second Coming the Jewish people would return to Zion and embrace Christianity. The restoration of the Jews was therefore for many a necessary prelude to the Second Coming. This belief was highly influential in succeeding centuries, especially in Britain and the United States. The nineteenth century saw variations, including dispensational premillennialism, initially propounded by the Plymouth Brethren, which held that during that millennium all Biblical prophecies would be realised through the Jewish people, once they had accepted Jesus as Messiah and king.

It was inevitable that the Zionist movement, from its foundation, should win a widespread following in those circles who saw it as a theological concept to be supported as a step towards the Second Coming and the conversion of the Jewish people. The establishment of the Jewish State of Israel fitted in perfectly with the evangelical timetable. 'If God has fulfilled His promise to Israel, then I feel He will keep His promise to me' was how one Evangelical clergyman expressed it to me, while the surge in evangelicanism in the past thirty years is partly attributed by some to the State of Israel, which provided a tangible proof of their eschatological schedule.

Today the Evangelical Churches are highly variegated and do not speak with one voice on Israel. The Evangelical Left, a small minority, is concerned about Palestinian Arab rights and tends to be supportive of Israel, though not uncritically. Their solidarity stems often more from a sense of justice for the Jewish people than for eschatological considerations, although these are not absent. The staunchest pro-Israel elements are to be found on the right of the Evangelical spectrum, stemming from their belief in the Biblical promise that God would bless those who blessed Israel and would curse those who cursed her. Developments in the Middle East are viewed through the lens of Biblical prophecy and are held to foreshadow the return of Jesus, Armageddon and the ultimate conversion of the Jews. They actively support Israel through media exposure, contributions, tourism and political action. They often identify with the hawkish Right in Israel's politics out of a similar belief that the divine promise related to the entire Land of Israel, no part of which should be surrendered. Leading Israelis, notably Menachem Begin, and Zionist groups have largely committed themselves to working with this segment of the Christian community.[23] For some of these Evangelicals, Israel is a main concern. There is, for example, a church in Denver, Colorado, with 7,000 members, nearly every one of whom has visited Israel, while Tulsa, Oklahoma, has an organisation called 'Goyyim for Israel'. Many of these Evangelicals identify personally with Israel, seeing themselves as some sort of continuity with the people of God. Their fundamentalist faith is often translated into a naive identification with Biblical prophecy.[24]

The enthusiasm for Israel on the part of such groups as the Moral Majority and the Evangelical Right poses problems for those many American Jews who oppose everything else these groups stand for – from their non-liberal stands on issues such as women's rights and abortion to their desired identification of Church and State to their Messianic and conversionist expectations and missionary fervour – but appreciate their willingness to go out on a limb for Israel, even on aspects that may be largely unpopular elsewhere in the American community (such as the war in Lebanon). Their dilemma can be epitomised by a recent study which showed that liberal Protestants in the U.S. scored relatively low on anti-Semitism and relatively high on unfriendliness to Israel while Evangelicals scored relatively high on anti-Semitism but also high on support for Israel.[25]

The Catholic Church and the State of Israel

When the entire city of Jerusalem came under Israeli rule in 1967, the Vatican had to accept the unpalatable fact that for the first time in history, all the Christian Holy Places now lay under Jewish control. The Israeli government, for its part, immediately sought to assuage reservations on this point by passing a law that guaranteed the protection of all the Holy Sites and ensured that there would be no change in their status.

The former solution of territorial internationalisation for Jerusalem was now dropped by the Vatican and replaced by a proposal for an internationally guaranteed statute for Jerusalem and the Holy Places. This remains Vatican policy, repeated on a number of occasions although remaining vague in formulation. It appears to advocate some form of control over Jerusalem's human and social structure, but to what part of the city it purports to apply has never been defined nor have the international auspices been envisaged. In any case, the concept is unacceptable to the Israeli authorities, who are unlikely to make concessions beyond the present situation which allows for a certain *de facto* autonomy within the strict confines of the Holy Places.

Israel was not mentioned in *Nostra Aetate* in 1965, in the 'Guidelines' of 1974 or in any papal statement before the 1980s (when the Israel Philharmonic Orchestra in the 1950s made a gesture to Pius XII by playing for him in the Vatican in recognition of what had been done by the Church to save Italian Jews in the Second World War, the official communiqué recorded that the Pope had 'received a group of Jewish refugee musicians'). Relations with Israel were especially strained in 1982 in the wake of the Pope's reception of Arafat. The Holy See has refused to establish any form of diplomatic relations with Israel or to accord it *de jure* recognition. The official explanations of its stand are based on political reasons, citing problems of non-finalised boundaries, Palestinian refugees, Lebanon, the West Bank and the status of Jerusalem as issues that must be resolved prior to full recognition, while there are continuing strong pressures from Muslim lands – including the Church in those countries – against any such move. Arguments from Jewish quarters pointing to inconsistencies in Vatican attitudes are brushed aside. Although official Catholic circles deny that theological factors are a consideration on this issue, it is difficult to believe that these have been totally eliminated, especially in the more conservative circles. Henry Siegman has written:

> The Vatican's refusal to establish normal diplomatic relations is arbitrary and deeply offensive. The Vatican has normal ties with the most oppressive and morally odious regimes. It maintained formal diplomatic ties with Nazi Germany until the very end of World War II. Apparently it considers only the State of Israel undeserving of its recognition. . . Its diplomacy persists in reflecting an anachronistic Catholic view that saw Jewish exile as punishment for Judaism's rejection of the message of Christianity. That old theology could not be reconciled with the return of Jewish sovereignty in Israel.[26]

Nevertheless, in many ways Vatican-Israel relations have improved over the past twenty years. Harbingers came from episcopal conferences. In 1975, the U.S. bishops recognised the Jewish tie to the Land of Israel and called on Christians to understand the link between the Land and the People,[27] while the Brazilian bishops in 1984 stated, as mentioned previously,

> God gave the ancient land of Canaan in which the Jews lived to Abraham and his descendant   We must recognise the rights of Jews to a calm political existence in their country of origin, without letting that create injustice or violence for other peoples. For the Jewish people these rights became reality in the State of Israel.[28]

In Rome, Popes began to receive Israeli leaders, while the Israeli embassy in Rome accredited a member of its staff charged exclusively with relations with the Vatican. In 1980, Pope John Paul II in a homily made the first public Papal reference to the State, saying that 'the Jewish people, after tragic experiences connected with the extermination of so many of its sons and daughters, driven by the desire for security, set up the State of Israel'.[29] In 1984, the Pope's Good Friday apostolic letter was devoted to 'the fate of the Holy City, Jerusalem'. This reaffirmed the Church's aforementioned claims in Jerusalem, also mentioning the Jewish and Muslim attachment to the city. Of especial significance was the statement: 'For the Jewish people who live in the State of Israel and preserve in that land such precious testimonies to their history and faith, we must ask for the desired security and the due tranquillity that is the prerogative of every nation and condition of life and of progress for every society.'[30] These sympathetic remarks, Vatican officials averred, were to be seen as a statement of *de facto* recognition of the State of Israel, although they were never issued through any diplomatic channels. Even more upbeat statements were being made by a number of cardinals particularly devoted to the fostering of Catholic–Jewish understanding. Thus, Cardinal Martini of Milan said: 'The hope that emerges from the Holocaust is the messianic promise of the land, of a reconciled land of Jerusalem, the city of peace, of a future world of messianic *Shalom*';[31] and the Dutch Cardinal Willebrands, head of the Vatican's Commission for Religious Relations with the Jews, stated: 'To carry the memory of many millions of deaths is a terrible burden; to have a place under the sun where to live in peace and security is a form of hope.'[32]

The third Vatican document on the Jews, the 1985 'Notes', contained elements of progress on this subject. The State of Israel was for the first time mentioned in an official Vatican document and recognition given to the continuing Jewish attachment to that land and its meaning for Jews. But it warns against Christians attributing religious significance to the link with the land.[33] This points up one of the basic ambivalences of this document and indeed of many Christian attitudes to Judaism and the Jews today. We are now often reminded of St. Paul's comment in Romans 11:29 that the gifts and the call of God are irrevocable, and the Notes enshrine the Pope's statement that the Old Covenant was never revoked. So are we speaking of one covenant or two? Does the second covenant incorporate and continue the first covenant or does it annul the first covenant? If, as has so long been held, the first covenant is annulled, then we are back where we began. But if, as is now indicated, the Old Covenant has never been revoked, does not this have to mean that it retains its validity as a whole? It is surely not being suggested that part of God's word is upheld and part is cancelled. If so, in the words of *The Times*'s editorial on the appearance of the Notes: 'If the concept of the Chosen People is still valid in Catholic teaching, why not also the concept of the Promised Land?'[34] The divine promise of the Land to the patriarchs and their descendants is an essential element of the covenant. The Notes reject the concept of a people punished so that the exile of the Jews should not be interpreted theologically. So how do we lose the Promised Land and why are Christians adjured not to see religious significance in the link of the People and the Land?

With reference to the State of Israel, the document says: 'The existence of the State of Israel and its political options should be envisaged not in a perspective which is itself religious but in their reference to the common principles of international law.' This opaque formulation has lent itself to various interpretations and one wonders what the teachers and preachers for whom it is intended will make of it, especially its vague citing of international law. Will they indeed remember that the State of Israel came into being as the result of a decision of the United Nations? And if the State is to be seen in the perspective of international law, how will they interpret the Vatican's withholding of formal recognition? In view of continuing attempts to delegitimate the State of Israel and continuing threats to its very existence, it had been hoped that the document would have clearly acknowledged the State's right to exist rather than this somewhat contorted formulation.

We have seen that the State of Israel remains one of the most problematic issues in the dialogue. The gap between the Jews' bond with it as part of their self-identity and the Christians' difficulty in assigning this religious meaning remains wide. The Christian theologian Roy Eckardt sees this in the broad context of Christian attitudes to Jews and Judaism:

> Overall Christian ambivalence to Zionism and the Jewish State reproduces the Christian ambivalence towards Judaism and Jewishness. The refusal or inability of some Christians to accept the State of Israel is a twentieth century variation upon the traditional Christian denial of Jewish rights and integrity. The treatment of Israel as a nation very largely recapitulates the treatment of the

Jewish people throughout Christian history.[35]

Some theologians are endeavouring to put the question of Israel into a new focus. The American Catholic, John Oesterreicher, notes the differences between the Jewish and Christian approaches to the Promised Land:

> To the Christian no land is holier than another. . . while it is difficult for the Christian to grasp the Jewish attachment to the Land, it does not forbid him to respect this attachment. There is no religious tenet that imposes on him a detached or neutral stance toward the reality that Jews have regained their own land and live under their own flag. . . I, at least, cannot see how the renewal of the land could be anything to the theologian but a wonder of love and vitality, how the reborn State could be anything but a sign of God's concern for His people.[36]

Father Flannery finds the Christians' reluctance to look upon the State of Israel with a full and open heart disappointing and surprising. The roots of this reluctance run in several directions, specifically into anti-Zionism, anti-Semitism and theological anti-Judaism. He writes that the chief obstacles to an accurate and full comprehension of Israel and its place in the Jewish-Christian interface have been (1) the politicisation of what is essentially a religious phenomenon, and (2) the mythologisation of that part of the phenomenon that is truly political. Further progress in the Jewish–Christian dialogue depends on the depoliticisation of the discussion on Israel and the demythologisation of the political opposition to that State. A Christian theology of Israel as a land hardly exists and will not make much headway without a more complete Christian theology of Judaism as well as a change in the inflamed atmosphere of the Middle East. He concludes that rather than theologising, what is needed is an authentic repentance for the contribution Christianity has made over the centuries to bring about the tragic rift between Christian and Jew, and to some degree also the impasse in the Middle East.[37]

Notes

1 *Commonweal*, 13 March 1987, p. 147.
2 D. Flusser in *Orot*, 14 (1973), p. 8.
3 T. F. Stransky in *America*, 8 February 1986, p. 93.
4 E. H. Flannery in *Face to Face*, Fall 1985, pp. 47-8.
5 S. Minerbi, *The Vatican, the Holy Land, and Zionism* (Hebrew), Jerusalem, 1986, p. 19.
6 M. Mendes, *The Vatican and Israel* (Hebrew), Jerusalem, 1983, p. 32.
7 *Ibid.*, pp. 36 ff.
8 S. Minerbi, *op. cit.* (see note 5), *passim*.
9 M. Pragai, *Faith and Fulfilment*, London, 1985, pp. 47-7.
10 See B. Tuchman, *Bible and Sword*, London, 1982.
11 L. Cremonesi in *Survey of Jewish Affairs, 1985*, ed. W. Frankel, London, 1985, p. 188.
12 *Stepping Stones to Further Jewish – Christian Relations*, ed. H. Kroner, New York, 1977, p. 71.
13 Cited in U. Tal, *The New Pattern in Jewish–Christian Dialogue*, (Hebrew), Jerusalem, 1969, p. 23.
14 *Stepping Stones* (see note 12), pp. 73ff.
15 Documents published by World Council of Churches, Programme Unit in Faith and Witness, March 1974.
16 See Appendix, pp. 00.
17 See A. R. Eckardt, *Jews and Christians*, Bloomington, 1986, p. 77.
18 M. Kramer, *Israel in the Muslim-Christian Dialogue*, Institute of Jewish Affairs Research Report, London, November 1986, Nos. 11-12, p. 2.
19 *Ibid.*, p. 18 (quoting *Muslim World*, 22 August 1981).
20 *Ibid.*, p. 20 (quoting *New Republic* (Washington), 4 February 1985).
21 This document does not appear to have been translated into English. I follow here the exposition of Uriel Tal in 'The New Pattern in Jewish-Christian Dialogue'(Hebrew), Jerusalem, 1969, citing *Israel und die Kirche: Eine Studie im Auftrag der Generalsynode der Niederlandischen Reformesten Kirche*, Zurich, 1961.
22 *Stepping Stones* (see note 12), pp. 91-107.
23 See Y. Eckstein, 'Understanding Evangelicals: a guide for the Jewish community', *Perspectives*, New York, May 1984.
24 On a lecture tour of evangelical groups in the U. S., I found a favourite question was 'When will the Third Temple be rebuilt?', and others wanted a confirmation of a report that when the original ashes of the Red Heifer are found, the Temple will have to be rebuilt. One questioner asked if it was true that the Hebrew University had instituted a course in sacrifice and that when the first graduates had qualified, the Temple would be rebuilt.
25 Y. Eckstein, *What Christians Should Know About Jews and Judaism*, Waco, 1984, p. 309.
26 *Congress Monthly*, February 1987, pp. 2,21.
27 *Stepping Stones* (see note 12), p. 34.
28 *More Stepping Stones to Jewish–Christian Relations*, ed. H. Kroner, New York, 1985, p. 153.
29 Quoted by E. H. Flannery in *Twenty Years of Jewish-Catholic Relations*, ed. E.

J. Fisher, A. J. Rudin and M. H. Tanenbaum, New York, 1986, p. 74.
30 *L'Osservatore Romano*, 20 April 1984.
31 *Christian – Jewish Relations*, Vol. 17, No. 4, December 1984, p. 5.
32 *Ibid.*, Vol 18 No. 1, March 1985, p. 27.
33 See Appendix, p. 000.
34 'The Old Covenant and the New', editorial, *The Times*, 1 July 1985.
35 A. R. Eckardt, *Jews and Christians*, Bloomington, 1986, p. 74.
36 Quoted by G. G. Higgins in *Twenty Years* (see note 29), p. 35.
37 *Twenty Years* (see note 36), pp. 76-85.

CHAPTER V

The dialogue in Israel

The interfaith dialogue in Israel is essentially an innovation introduced by Jews and Christians of Western origin. The long history of the Holy Land has been characterised by the most unholy interreligious disputes with interfaith understanding conspicuous by its absence. The three great monotheistic faiths with special interests in Israel are not in themselves monolithic and interreligious hostility has been compounded by intra-religious strife and rivalries. In particular the history of the Christian presence in the Holy Land has been characterised by internal frictions, especially over control of the Holy Places.[1] The situation is even more difficult and complex in our own time because of the many tensions that bedevil the area. All the country's Muslims and almost all its Christians are Arabs with deep senses of grievance and criticism concerning the Jews and these cannot be shut out when it comes to interreligious contacts, especially as for the Muslims – as for Jews – the religious sphere embraces ethnic aspects. Moreover, for geographical reasons, the main population of each group lives in a certain isolation from the other so that most Jews, for example, have no meaningful contact with non-Jews and retain their stereotypes undisturbed.[2]

Absentees from the dialogue

Ideally, we should be speaking in Israel of a trialogue and indeed a number of individual Muslims are involved in interfaith frameworks in the country. But, as has been noted, the problem of dialogue with Islam is worldwide as it is still largely bound and guided by medieval theological concepts, especially reinforced in the Middle East by the rapid growth of fundamentalist forces. Some attempts at trialogue have been made in the West but in Israel, at any rate, open theological dialogue with Islam is virtually non-existent. This situation has been made even more difficult by the absence of an intellectual religious leadership among Israel's Muslims; in 1948, the Muslim religious leaders in the country left for Egypt and Syria and the intellectuals among the younger Muslim generations in Israel have entered spheres of life other than religion.

Among Christians, certain Churches are also outside the dialogue as a result of a medieval mentality and fundamentalism. The Orthodox and Eastern Churches remain closed not only to interfaith dialogue but to significant ecumenical co-operation with other Christian churches in the country. The Uniate Churches, notably the Greek Catholics, have been largely untouched by the revolution of the Vatican Council and some in Israel resent the positive changes that have occurred in the relationship between other branches of Christianity and the Jews. The Arab Christians feel no responsibility for the Holocaust nor do they display any understanding that their traditional teachings and liturgies have contributed to anti-Semitism. As Arabs they, like the Muslims, feel themselves the innocent victims of the West's resolution of its guilt feelings over the Holocaust by supporting the establishment of the State of Israel. For most indigenous Christians in the Middle East, their loyalty to their Arab identity precludes compromise with the State of Israel and with a Judaism involving the Return to Zion. They are sensitive even to Biblical mentions of 'Israel' which they tend to identify with the modern Jewish claim to the State of Israel, and their hierarchy tends to support Palestinian nationalism. Many Arab Christians and Muslims reject interfaith which they see as a codeword for a hidden agenda aimed at securing the political understanding they so resolutely oppose. There is thus really no dialogue with the Eastern Churches and, should it develop, it cannot be along the same lines as that with the Western churches in view of their absence of theological sophistication – even to the very language

used, to their long minority experience, and to their ethnic iden-
tifications and preoccupations, often incorporating anti-Jewish
theologies and attitudes.

The perspective of the entire Middle Eastern maze must also
be remembered, notably the experience of the past dozen years
in Lebanon from which Christians have drawn far-reaching
lessons. They are acutely aware of their growing marginality in
the entire region where the upsurge of Muslim fundamentalism
has made their situation increasingly precarious. The conclusion
drawn by many Christians, particularly among the younger
generations, is to emigrate from the Middle East, where they are
doomed to a minority status, and move elsewhere, preferably to
the Western Hemisphere, where they can become part of Christian majorities. An exodus of Christians is part of the regular
pattern throughout the area, even though in Israel their absolute
numbers continue to rise as a result of their high birth-rate.

Prominent in the dialogue are Western Christians living in
Israel, but they are a tiny and often transient group. Where they
minister to a local flock, their interfaith interests may have to be
tempered as a result of the opposition of their congregants who
may view their involvement in dialogue with suspicion or even
hostility. However, their role can be innovative by the injection
of fresh perspectives, such as modernity into a world of tradition
or ecumenism into habitual isolation.

The fundamentalism to which we have referred in connection with Islam and eastern Christianity is no less a growing
phenomenon among Orthodox Jews and nowhere more so than
in Israel. Individual Orthodox Jews are involved in interfaith
dialogue and activities but they are a small minority. The majority,
including the religious establishment, are wary of, or opposed to,
dialogue. For some the objections run along the lines explained
in Chapter II which traced the general reservations of the
Orthodox to the interfaith encounter; for others, the missionary
trauma is uppermost. Those who take their fundamentalism to
extremes display the same medieval ways of thinking as those
encountered among the Muslims and Eastern Christians. In
recent years, the power of these extremist Jews has grown

immensely within the overall framework of Jewish religious Orthodoxy and consequently on the political scene. Their strategic position is such that neither the left nor right bloc of parties struggling for ascendancy dare offend them. They do, it is true, support religious pluralism (as long as it is not applied within Judaism to non-Orthodox trends) but this is not only for its ideological value but also out of the expedient consideration of the situation of their fellow Jews, especially the Orthodox, living in Christian or Muslim lands. Many religious and nationalist elements have been seized by a newly-acquired note of triumphalism, with its vindication of the Jewish version of Messianism, which ever since the beginning of the Exile was associated with the return of the Jews to their own Land (and many Orthodox Jews have now added to their prayers references to the State of Israel as the 'beginning of redemption'). When the Jew was confined to his ghetto, his Messianism brought him comfort and hope in his situation of powerlessness; but to be motivated by Messianism when in a position of power is fraught with danger and can – and does – engender intolerance. An important role is played by internal religious rivalries within the Jewish Orthodox ranks, which incorporate a broad variety of sects and groups, each trying to outdo the other. The result has been the victory of extremism and the heresy of moderation. Many manifestations must be seen against this background, including anti-missionary excesses, the campaign against the opening in Jerusalem of a branch of Utah's Mormon Brigham Young University, demonstrations against archaeological digs, and – potentially most dangerous – attempts to establish a Jewish presence on the Temple Mount, regarded by the Muslims with the most intense zeal as one of their great Holy Places. Those working to cultivate understanding between faiths and communities live in trepidation of acts of fanaticism from all sides, which in a minute can undermine and destroy years of patient bridge-building.

Finally in this roster of fundamentalists outside the dialogue in Israel, mention must be made of the Christian Evangelicals, many with open or concealed conversionist objectives. These groups are very varied and, for the most part, tiny, and some on the liberal wing do participate in dialogue. Their most publicised activity was the establishment in Jerusalem in September 1980 of the 'International Christian Embassy'. This followed the condemnation by the UN of Israel's 'Jerusalem Law' as a result of which all embassies situated in Jerusalem moved to Tel Aviv. As a gesture of identification with the State of Israel and Jerusalem, its capital, a group of Evangelical Christians took over one of the vacated embassies and set up the 'International Christian Embassy' which has developed a variety of programmes inside Israel with outreach projects to sympathisers around the world. However, for the majority, interfaith or even ecumenical activity is not on their agenda. Their form of fundamentalism, with its literal acceptance and interpretation of Holy Writ, does not admit the note of compromise assumed by dialogue. Where they work with peoples of other faiths, their hope – proximate or ultimate – is to win them to their beliefs, and their targets are not only Jews but Muslims and even Christians of other persuasions. It should be remarked that a survey made a few years ago showed that only 10 out of 160 Christian religious and social services communities in Israel have an open interest in proselytisation, and none of these is affiliated with any major Christian denomination.[3]

Attitudes to mission

While Israel in its framework as a pluralistic democracy recognises missionary activity as an authentic expression of faith, the problem is the achievement of a balance between freedom of denominational action and the sensibilities of the majority community. Does responsibility for intercommunal harmony rest solely with the majority community or should not the minorities accept some of the responsibility and carefully consider the potential consequences of their activities? And may not the majority draw a line when it comes to certain minority groups such as 'Moonies' and Scientologists – and if so, where is such a line to be drawn? Questions such as these emerge from missionary activities and the sensitivities are not confined to the majority group, the Jews; the Christians and Muslims are suspicious of the Mormons, the

Greeks and Latins oppose the Protestant missionaries, and so on.

In Jewish circles, Christian missionising gives offence beyond Orthodox circles. Inasmuch as Judaism is an ethnic as well as a religious category, attempts to remove Jews from Judaism are seen by some as attempts to detach Jews from their peoplehood and hence a virtual incitement to treachery. Claims that Jews can leave their faith for Christianity and still remain members of the Jewish people are not accepted by Jews, even if justification could be found in the Jewish legal principle that 'However much a Jew sins, he remains a Jew.' In any case, we are repeatedly being reminded of the tastelessness of missionary efforts in the generation after the Holocaust when the reservoir of Jewish manpower has contracted so massively. For many Jews, notably those of European descent and especially among the Orthodox elements who have remained ghettoised in Israel, the diaspora missionary trauma – fruit of centuries of bitter conditioning – has remained overpowering. In 1978, the ultra-Orthodox Agudat Israel party sought to introduce an anti-missionising bill into Israel's parliament. When they realised their proposal had no support, they retreated and modified the bill to outlaw the offering of bribes to anyone to change their religion (and as this was left in general terms, it could theoretically apply to attempts to win converts to any faith, including Judaism, through material inducements). In these terms the bill is unobjectionable, and indeed accords with declarations along similar lines by major Christian denominations. However in view of the original intentions of the movers, the Christian community felt considerable unease. They were reassured by the Attorney-General, who promised that no prosecution would be instigated without his personal investigation and approval, and indeed the bill has never been invoked. But in view of the new muscle of the ultra-Orthodox, restrictive legislative initiatives are not beyond the bounds of possibility.

Numerically the greatest success of the missionaries has been among other Christian denominations. The number of Jews converting is tiny – during the State's first twenty years it averaged six a year and does not seem to have become significantly higher, although exaggerated figures are often quoted by Jewish anti-missionary organisations. Certainly far more Christians in Israel have converted to Judaism, encouraged by government-sponsored instruction courses.

Different emphases can be discerned in Christian attitudes to proselytisation. At one end of the spectrum are the high-powered missionaries, affiliated with evangelical churches. The less highly-motivated accept the Christian hope for Jewish conversion but feel it inappropriate to take action in the current situation. A third and most sophisticated – but probably the smallest – group rejects even the proselytisation ideal and acknowledges Judaism as a way to God. These Christians seek to work together with Jews in an atmosphere of reconciliation and respect. A pragmatic approach on the issue was advocated by Eugene Carson Blake when General Secretary of the World Council of Churches: 'Our concern in Israel should be voiced in terms of service rather than mission. Mission, in the sense of Christian witness, is in Israel a very dirty word. It is understood by Jews exclusively in terms of proselytising.'[4]

A Jewish reaction has been expressed by Shemaryahu Talmon, one of the principal exponents of Jewish–Christian dialogue in Israel:

> Once the admitted 'permanence' of the other's religion is agreed upon, it is obvious that the aim of dialogue must be to become better informed of each other's tenets and beliefs to work out a system of livable coexistence. This admittedly does not exclude the possibility of conversions. Anybody who willingly enters into a dialogue takes the risk of having his ideas influenced. But the dialogue situation imposes on us the obligation to curb any attempts at exploiting the situation of the underprivileged for the furthering of missionary aims.[5]

Interfaith activities

Despite all these problems, Israel is the scene of fruitful activity and dialogue. The first tentative gropings were made in the pre-State period, under the leadership of distinguished thinkers such as Martin Buber and Hugo Bergmann. It achieved organisational expression in the late 1950s with the establishment of the Israel

Interfaith Committee (later, Association), which now has a membership of Jews, Christians, Muslims and Druze with branches in a number of towns. Two influential theological workshops dating from the 1960s are the Christian Ecumenical Theological Research Fraternity, whose research concentrates on the study of Judaism and the theological implications for Christians of the State of Israel, and the Rainbow Group, which brings together Jewish and Christian thinkers (and which has inspired similar groups in London and New York). A considerable number of bodies and projects are working on interfaith and intercommunal projects; some are engaged in theological interchange, others in educational programming, others in the development of mutual understanding by fostering social encounter. The scene in Jerusalem is enriched by a considerable number of students who attend Christian institutions to study the Bible and archaeology and the Jewish background of the New Testament and early Christianity, often with Jewish scholars.[6]

The fostering of interfaith understanding is an uphill struggle, having to contend with the forces of obscurantism, nationalism and fanaticism. Numerically those actively involved are not large and reflect a similar assymetry to that noted in the West. The Jews engaged tend to be motivated primarily by historical and pragmatic considerations while the Christians include many clerics – mostly of Western origin – for whom the relationship with Judaism is a fundamental theological consideration. However, none of the establishments is involved; the Chief Rabbis, Muftis and Patriarchs do not meet and the religious institutions are all inwardly-directed.

Christians in dialogue in Israel recognise the continuing validity of the link between the Jews and their land. For them the rebirth of Israel is a deep mystery with profound theological implications. Indeed, some have gone to Israel for the express purpose of trying to fathom this mystery. The vitality of the State and of the Jewish people in their land confirms for them God's faithfulness to His covenant people, with great significance for Christianity. Some of the Evangelicals, as the natural conclusion of their millenarianism, have been led to endorse Jewish rule over the whole Land of Israel to the Jordan river – and perhaps even beyond – as confirming the restoration of the Jews to the biblical boundaries of the Promised Land.

The dialogue agenda in Israel, as elsewhere, is both theological and practical. The latter is devoted to building bridges and also to fighting prejudice and discrimination and upholding social justice. The theological aspects stress the Jewish link with the Land through covenant and history, the Christian links with the Land through the life of Jesus and the Jewish roots of Christianity. One novel aspect for the Christians is that for the first time in history (apart from the first decades of Christianity), they are living as a Christian minority within a Jewish majority. This turning of the historical tables has much to teach both sides. The Jews, they feel, can learn from the Church's experience of power, especially its errors, while the Christians have a great deal to derive, both positively and negatively, from the long Jewish experience as a minority. Moreover the latter consideration is increasingly relevant to the Christian situation in many parts of the world. Christianity is no longer in the dominant position it held for so many centuries, leading one Israeli to dub interfaith as 'a partnership of losers'.[7] For the Jews in Israel, a broad perspective taking in the entire Middle East, points up their continuing minority situation, a tiny island in a Muslim sea, and this should – in the words of Shemaryahu Talmon – 'take the sting out of hubris and triumphalism'. He has added that the positive side of the Israel interfaith scene is the proof of the interpenetration of the social, political and theological dimensions. Theology cannot be contemplated solely on the abstract scholarly plane but must act itself out in the realities of group life and individual life. The new possibilities offer a better understanding of the religion – history – people – land complex which has always typified Judaism and is also to be found to some degree in certain eastern Churches, such as the Armenian.[8]

What goes by the name of religion has had a long record in the Holy Land as a major cause of conflict, distrust, persecution and discrimination. It would have been a far more tranquil, if less inspiring and stimulating, region without its religious associations. We are justified in wondering whether at this stage it is realistic to expect religion to be transformed from an obstacle in the way of peace to an instrument of reconciliation. All indications are that such a turn is highly unlikely. We are faced with three world religions with – in the Middle East at any rate – highly particularistic messages which drown out universalist nuances and the modest attempts at the fostering of interfaith understanding appear little more than a potential growth or a palliative. One Western Christian who occupied a key interfaith role in Jerusalem for a number of years, Coos Schoneveld, concluded his term of office with the words:

> Are Judaism, Christianity and Islam mutually exclusive religions which are in everlasting strife and competition among themselves? Christianity and Islam both have their theories of substitution and suppression of other religions, albeit in different ways. If this is their last answer, then the future is very black and we have to despair of religion as a contributing factor to peace.[9]

Certainly from Jerusalem the perspective is very different from in the more sophisticated West. Sermons and ecclesiastical pronouncements throughout the Middle East tend not to be the sometimes platitudinous endorsements of generally accepted ethical principles so often heard in the West but – especially in Islam – bitter incitement and denunciations, deeply involved with political issues. The mosques not infrequently resound to the call to a Holy War. Those who speak of dialogue and interfaith are regarded in these quarters as effete do-gooders, at worst as promoting Western colonial interests.

But there are levels at which results are being achieved and it is these that give hope. Some of this in Israel is expressed in terms of personal encounter; for others, it is on the ideological plane. We have used the term 'interfaith', but often this is misleading in our Jewish–Christian context, especially in Israel. For the practicing Christian, the aspect of faith is clear, but for many Jews this is less easy to define. Judaism of the post-Emancipation vintage is of a complex nature combining various elements, each of which itself may be dispensable without detracting from a Jewish identity. Many Jews would deny they had 'faith' in the Christian religious sense but would not be inhibited from participation in an interfaith framework. The concept of 'interfaith' becomes complicated as the Christians may comprehend that their counterparts' credo may be expressed in a secular culture or through identification with a physical land but they find it difficult to relate where there is no religious faith or where theology is replaced by history or sociology. However, the growing awareness of the compound character of Judaism (or Jewishness) has cleared away many hoary misconceptions and provides a potential paradigm for a far broader understanding of interfaith, with a relevance not confined to Israel.

One of the Christians involved has described the Israel interfaith experience as a unique opportunity to examine one's own faith 'and discover the difference between what is essential and what is mere cultural heritage'.[10] Others are now convinced that the roots of Christianity are not only enriched but unthinkable without contact with the living Jewish people in its land. Here they feel they can come closest to the living experience of Jesus in an all-Jewish environment in which Saturday is the Sabbath day, the Jewish holidays are days of rest and observance, and the language spoken is the Hebrew tongue redolent of the Bible and the language of the early sages.

Some of the Christians involved in Israel interfaith are respected thinkers with international reputations and through them the impact of the encounter reaches wide Church circles. One of the most prominent dialogue personalities is Marcel Dubois, a Dominican priest who is chairman of the Department of Philosophy at the Hebrew University (in itself a noteworthy manifestation of the new relationship, especially when it is recalled that the Dominicans were the Fathers of the Inquisition). In his writings he has conveyed the special flavour of the encounter in Israel. For example:

> In the destiny of Israel, in that of the people of the Bible and also of the Jews throughout history, we see the exemplary figure of the spiritual destiny of Man and we read the Scriptures in this light. We discover more and more plainly that the inheritance of Israel is one of the elements of Christian identity. We respect Jewish

subjectivity and place ourselves in its angle to understand Israel's actual demeanour and vouchsafe to the Jewish soul to be faithful to its own identity. In this perspective, the return to Zion seems to imply a return to God, or, at least, allegiance to a mysterious vocation of which Christians rejoice to be the most attentive and exigent witness.[11]

Notes

1 See J. Parkes, *History of Palestine* London, 1949; S. P. Colbi, *Christianity in the Holy Land*, Jerusalem, 1969; W. Zander, *Israel and the Holy Places of Christendom*, London, 1971.

2 For a fuller discussion of this chapter, see G. Wigoder in *When Jews and Christians Meet*, ed. J. J. Petuchowski, New York, 1988. Also G. Wigoder, *Interfaith Dialogue in Israel*, Research Report, Institute of Jewish Affairs, London, June 1983 and in *Christian–Jewish Relations*, Vol. 19 No. 3, September 1986, pp. 7-15.

3 According to a 1982 breakdown of the Christian population of Israel, there were 73,080 Roman Catholics, 43,170 Orthodox, 4,600 Monophysites, and 4,150 Protestants.

4 *Church and Society*, July – August 1972.

5 'Interfaith Dialogue', special supplement of *Immanuel*, Autumn 1973.

6 For fuller details see *Christian–Jewish Relations* (note 2).

7 'Interfaith Dialogue' (note 5).

8 *Ibid.*

9 C. Schoneveld in *Christianity in the Holy Land*, ed. D. M. A. Jaeger, Tantur, Jerusalem, 1981, pp. 277-88.

10 A. Rainey in 'Christian Comment', *Jerusalem Post*, 30 May, 1975.

11 *Christian News from Israel*, Spring 1973.

AFTERWORD

Our survey has encompassed a mere forty years, a tiny time-span in which to eradicate the accumulation of mistrust and hatred built up over nineteen centuries. Dialogue is a new religious experience with no precedents for guidance, certainly within a Christian – Jewish context. Mistakes have been made and inevitably many suspicions remain, together with residues of prejudice on either side. Nevertheless, the outstanding conclusion is that positive foundations that appear to be solid, have been laid.

Various propositions have emerged as basic to the new Christian–Jewish relationship:

1. The goal is mutual understanding and appreciation based on what we have in common with respect for where we differ. What we have in common includes joint roots, and the monotheistic faith with its ethical and social corollaries, including the principle of human brotherhood.

2. The Jewish way to God is not the Christian way to God, nor is the Christian way to God the Jewish way. We recognise the right of the other to its own way and we seek no form of syncretism.

3. The Jewish–Christian relationship is based on the acceptance of the principle of equality between the two faiths, the prerequisite for true encounter.

4. Our mutual understanding is founded on the self-definition of the other which we seek to comprehend but not to change.

5. Inevitably, the dialogue is assymetrical. For Christianity, the relationship to Judaism has elements of dependency and causality absent from the Jewish relationship to Christianity. Jews, for their part, have special expectations in view of the long history of Christian anti-Semitism. At the same time, Jewish thinkers are now called on to face the world of Christian ideas.

The Christian–Jewish encounter is being conducted at various levels. The pathfinders are often the individual theologians grappling with new realities and insights. Their theoretical originality often has practical implications and applications. Belief and practice have always been indivisible in Jewish tradition and are becoming increasingly intertwined in the Christian world, Catholic and Protestant. The establishments are called on to set the tone for the masses of believers but traditionally are conservative by nature. In the post-war world, especially as a response to external challenges, the Western establishments have been willing to discard long-standing traditions and embrace revisionist, liberal doctrines, among them positive approaches to ecumenical and interfaith developments. In this they have in many cases been prodded by the theologians on the one hand and on the other, by initiatives taken by lower establishments (for example, in the Catholic world, initiatives of national episcopal bodies have put pressure on the Vatican). Finally, we now have the laymen and those at grassroots level who usually tend to continue in their furrow unless leads are given from above. In some cases, however, demands from the laymen do percolate upwards although in Jewish–Christian dialogue the Establishment has generally taken the lead. Revisions in religious teaching have been partially responsible for the great changes that have occurred but recognition must be made of the impact of the acceptance of pluralism, as well as of the mass media, which have punctured stereotypes such as the traditional anti-Semitic image of the Jew by bringing the living Jew and even Judaism into every home.

As we have seen, both the Christian and the Jewish world are far from monolithic. However, all Christians, like all Jews, have a shared base and, despite the diversities, have much in common; for Christians this includes the conviction of the universality of the Christian orientation as well as the experience of long centuries of negation of – or of professing a basic negative attitude to – Jewish identity. The tempering of triumphalism is a trauma for the Churches in the post-war world, calling for profound theological revisions, of which the attitude to Jews and Judaism is only one aspect.

From a Jewish perspective, the Christian view of the Jews is still beset by major problems:

1. *Anti-Semitism.* Much significant achievement in recent

decades has been accomplished on this subject and without doubt the Western Churches have succeeded in eliminating many sources, especially of a cruder nature, of anti-Jewish prejudice. Moreover, openness to the reading of the Old Testament and the teaching of the Jewish roots of Christianity and the Jewishness of Jesus have led to revisions of many deeply held presuppositions and prejudices. But the underlying root of these teachings has still to be contended with. The literal story of the Crucifixion in the New Testament as well as the indoctrination, explicit or implicit, of belief in supersessionism must continue to foster negative attitudes towards Jews and Judaism. However much anti-Semitism is condemned at one level, its seeds remain in place at the other and Christians are called upon to face the paradox of condemning something they theologically justify.

2. *The role of Jews and Judaism after the coming of Jesus and in salvation history.* Discontinuity has been taken for granted for so long that it would not be realistic to expect belief in it to disappear overnight. Some Christian theologians have faced the problem and new interpretations have been proposed for Romans 9-11, challenging the familiar view, but these have not reached large areas of Christendom. Discontinuity for the Christian is a coherent element in his theological *Weltanschauung* and its replacement by continuity demands a considerable degree of sophistication. Christianity retains an innate triumphalism, and even though attempts have been made to temper this and at least to remove it to the eschatological plane, non-Christians remain unconvinced and uncertain of the salvific hope of the Churches. Strangely, the very special nature of the relationship with the Jews means that the hope that they will 'enter into the fullness' is stronger and more lasting than such expectation for the 'heathen' nations. Jews seeking to discover the Churches' ultimate ideal for the Jews do not receive answers congruent with their own self-definition.

3. *Mission.* Linked to the previous point is the need for the relationship to be totally detached from mission to be acceptable to Jews. Mission in general implies intolerance and a rejection of that pluralism today broadly accepted in Western societies. For

137

Jews it is particularly offensive for both theological and historical reasons. Christians must realise that Jews cannot accept Jesus as Lord and Messiah and that for Judaism God cannot be mediated, only interpreted – a role played by the Torah. The Catholic Church's endorsement of the distinction between witness and unwarranted proselytism and its abandonment of mission to the Jews constitute a historic step forward in the Christian–Jewish encounter. The possibility of change of faith in either direction may be the result of open dialogue but this is a legitimate consequence of a free society and is very different from organised attempts at proselytism.

4. *Israel.* While the Jews' yearning for a return to their ancient homeland has always been integral to Judaism, it has acquired a new urgency and priority as a result of the experience of the Holocaust and the establishment of the State of Israel. The Jewish dialogue expectation is for Christian recognition of this essential element of their self-definition. The response is not always easy, as the relationship of covenant to Land and Jews to Israel is strange to the Christian mind. Politically Christians may – or may not – react sympathetically but the problem is how to digest it theologically. The question does not arise for the Evangelical Churches for whom the course of events harmonises perfectly with their eschatology. Nor does it arise for those Christians who continue to maintain a belief in discontinuity and the abrogation of God's covenant with Israel and for whom therefore the Jews have no religious claim to the Land. But in the major dialogues we have been discussing, Israel remains a perplexing, controversial, and sometimes divisive issue. One hurdle that has been to a large extent overcome in these contexts is the belief that the exile of the Jews was a punishment for their rejection of Jesus. This teaching was so entrenched that its total eradication within a few years was not a realistic expectation. But today it is seldom expressed or taught to the younger generations, at any rate in the West where, it is to be hoped, it will soon be little more than a historical footnote. However, its retention in certain conservative circles may still be having an effect on attitudes and policies concerning the State of Israel.

Both the Vatican and the World Council of Churches have come round in the 1980s to speaking in official documents of the religious significance for Jews of their attachment to the Land. But concerning Christians they have either denied religious significance to this attachment or avoided grappling with the question. The problem arises as a result of the reaffirmation of the validity of the first covenant, to which the Divine promise of the Land is integral, and consequently the view of the return of the Jews to Zion as an expression of divine faithfulness.

The issue is the Jewish link with the Land and the Return to Zion rather than the political State of Israel which cannot claim religious endorsement from Christians in itself but only as a manifestation of the Return. For those accepting the religious aspect of the Return, it follows that the Jews who have resettled their Land must be motivated not only by political considerations and the aspiration to normalisation but also must accept covenant obligations, the nature of which are seen differently by Christians and Jews. The former view them in universal terms which to the Jews are unrealistic and a distortion of the covenant. But for Jews who see the Return in covenantal terms, there are ritual and ethical responsibilities as well as the duty to be, in the words of the Bible, 'a beacon to the gentiles'. This would apply, for example, to attitudes to Palestinian Arabs, which should not be expressed in terms of 'evenhanded' balancing as has been the case in many Church documents, but should be seen as an articulation of the social justice demanded of Jews in their land as part of the covenant.

Turning now to Jewish attitudes to the dialogue, it has been noted that the diverse forms of Judaism preclude a unanimity of approach also on the Jewish side. Jewish sensitivities, heightened by the Holocaust, are now uttered more openly, while post-war developments, including the acceptance of all forms of pluralism and the emergence of the State of Israel, have engendered a new self-confidence among Diaspora Jews, who see themselves no longer as a minority, with implications of inferiority, but as one out of various ethnic elements comprising the country in which they live. The resultant self-assertiveness, a new phenomenon in

Diaspora history, has been beneficial to the dialogue as for the first time the Christian–Jewish relationship can be conducted under conditions of equality and impartiality. It is because of this new state of affairs that Orthodox Jewish authorities have felt it necessary to impose certain constraints, although their exclusion of 'faith commitments' from the dialogue is hard to implement in Judaism where no concern is purely secular and no distinction is drawn between the City of God and the City of Man.

Although Jews (notably Franz Rosenzweig and Martin Buber) pioneered the new relationship, in the post-war world the initiative has been taken by the Christians. Much of the Jewish population remains in a state of voluntary intellectual ghettoisation, retaining the Jewish stereotypes of Christians and Christian attitudes, preserving the picture, justified over so many centuries, that the Christian is inherently anti-Semitic (and, by extension, anti-Israel) without a clear examination of whether changes have really occurred. The Jewish media (including the Israeli media), for example, continue to place great emphasis on any anti-Semitic manifestation while tending to ignore philo-Semitic expressions. The new-found triumphalism of certain Jewish right-wing Orthodox and nationalist circles is detrimental to any form of moderation, including interfaith understanding. At the same time, extensive progress has resulted from basic changes in the Jewish world. The intensive academisation of the Jews has brought a very high proportion into a world where they examine the intellectual values of others while the above mentioned pluralism, while enabling those who so wish to live an internalised life undisturbed, also leads to respect for the other and a determination to remove areas of friction and promote fraternal coexistence.

Crucial for the future is the role of education. A leading Vatican educator recently stated[1] that he is alarmed at the retention of anti-Jewish prejudices in textbooks submitted for his approval. In his case, these were promptly eliminated, but they still appear elsewhere. But the trend of forty years has been to weed out anti-Jewish prejudices, although not enough is being done in either Jewish or Christian education to build up a respectful understanding of the values and beliefs of the other. The presentation of Christianity in Jewish education is still primarily restricted to the long history of Christian anti- Semitism while Christian textbooks largely ignore any mention of post-Biblical Judaism, the post-Biblical history of the Jews, anti-Semitism in general and its Christian implications in particular.

The Israeli scholar David Flusser has summed up as follows:

> Many principles and ideas are common to both religions. Not only belief in one and the same personal God and in the Old Testament past, but even the mode of religious creative thought bears similarities. The manner of argumentation is often alike and it should be easy to see that this is not accidental. Christians should therefore be actually seized by curiosity to learn how Judaism was carried on and how it developed those beginnings which Christianity too adopted in its early days. This holy curiosity should extend to such situations where it is not a question of transfer from Judaism to Christianity but a mutual, parallel development, independent of interaction. Christianity's gain from post-Christian Judaism is quite evident in this case. The same applies to Jewish ideas on faith, on messianism and eschatology, and on the Jewish hope for redemption.
>
> There are situations when Judaism has greater experience than Christianity and its theology rests on surer foundations. yet the reverse holds true as well. Judaism can learn a great deal from Christian treatment of common problems. Judaism and Christianity could be likened to two students with similar backgrounds who have been assigned the same tasks,. It is fitting that these two should not keep from each other their experience and attempts at solutions but should rather help each other.[2]

It has been suggested that the dialogue has reached its theoretical limit and that no further change is possible;[3] the Churches by now have defined their positions in the new circumstances while the Jews have also made their stands clear. A line may have been reached which neither side wishes to overstep. This may signal a coming of age of the dialogue and a need to change direction, with the main emphasis being directed at deepening rather than broadening the new relationship.

In today's world, our situation is one of growing interdependence as we both face not only the external threat of secularism and atheism but the internal dangers of conservatism and fundamentalism. From this vantage point Christians and Jews committed to dialogue and interfaith understanding sit on the same side of the fence. The challenge now is to ensure that the lessons derived and the values developed in recent decades are not isolated in a few pockets but are brought to general grassroots acceptance. The stress should be on our common heritage and aspirations rather than the sometimes masochistic harpings on the ills of the past, although these must not be forgotten as object lessons. A little light dispels much darkness and as our survey of four decades has shown, new validations have been discovered for the hope that characterises both faiths.

Notes

1 Monsignor Pietro Rossano, Rector of the Pontifical Lateran University, Rome, in an address in Jerusalem, 1987.
2 D. Flusser in C. Thoma, *A Christian Theology of Judaism*, New York, 1980, pp. 10-12.
3 See A. Hertzberg in *Christian–Jewish Relations*, Vol. 18 No. 3, September 1985, p. 21 (Hertzberg is referring here specifically to the Jewish – Catholic dialogue.)

APPENDIX: DOCUMENTS

I Statements by Vatican authorities

Vatican II on the Jews. Nostra Aetate *(n. 4), October 1965. This conciliar statement is part of the Declaration on the Relationship of the Church to Non-Christian Religions.*

As this Council searches into the mystery of the Church, it remembers the bond that spiritually ties the people of the New Covenant to Abraham's stock.

Thus the Church of Christ acknowledges that, according to God's saving design, the beginnings of her faith and her election are found already among the Patriarchs, Moses and the prophets. She professes that all who believe in Christ – Abraham's sons according to faith – are included in the same Patriarch's call, and likewise that the salvation of the Church is mysteriously foreshadowed by the chosen people's exodus from the land of bondage. The Church, therefore, cannot forget that she received the revelation of the Old Testament through the people with whom God in His inexpressible mercy concluded the Ancient Covenant. Nor can she forget that she draws sustenance from the root of that well-cultivated olive tree onto which has been grafted the wild shoot, the Gentiles. Indeed, the Church believes that by His cross Christ Our Peace reconciled Jews and Gentiles, making both one in Himself.

The Church keeps ever in mind the words of the Apostle about his kinsmen: 'Theirs is the sonship and the glory and the covenants and the law and the worship and the promises; theirs are the fathers and from them is the Christ according to the flesh' (Rom 9:4-5), the Son of the Virgin Mary. She also recalls that the Apostles, the Church's mainstay and pillars, as well as most of the early disciples who proclaimed Christ's Gospel to the world, sprang from the Jewish people.

As Holy Scripture testifies, Jerusalem did not recognize the time of her visitation, nor did the Jews, in large number, accept the Gospel; indeed not a few opposed its spreading. Nevertheless God holds the Jews most dear for the sake of their Fathers; He does not repent of the gifts He makes or of the calls He issues – such is the witness of the Apostle. In company with the Prophets and the same Apostle, the Church awaits that day, known to God alone, on which all peoples will address the Lord in a single voice and 'serve Him with one accord' (Zeph 3:9).

Since the spiritual patrimony common to Christians and Jews is thus so great, this Council wants to foster and recommend that mutual understanding and respect which is the fruit, above all, of Biblical and

143

theological studies as well as of fraternal dialogues.

True, the Jewish authorities and those who followed their lead pressed for the death of Christ; still, what happened in His passion cannot be charged against all the Jews, without distinction, then alive, nor against the Jews of today. Although the Church is the new people of God, the Jews should not be presented as rejected or accursed by God, as if this followed from the Holy Scriptures. All should see to it, then, that in catechetical work or in the preaching of the word of God they do not teach anything that does not conform to the truth of the Gospel and the spirit of Christ.

Furthermore, in her rejection of every persecution against any man, the Church, mindful of the patrimony she shares with the Jews and moved not by political reasons but by the Gospel's spiritual love, decries hatred, persecutions, displays of anti-Semitism, directed against Jews at any time and by anyone.

Besides, as the Church has always held and holds now, Christ underwent His passion and death freely, because of the sins of men and out of infinite love, in order that all may reach salvation. It is, therefore, the burden of the Church's preaching to proclaim the cross of Christ as the sign of God's all-embracing love and as the fountain from which every grace flows.

Guidelines and Suggestions for Implementing the Conciliar Declaration Nostra Aetate (n. 4), by the Vatican Commission for Religious Relations with the Jews, January 1975.

The Declaration *Nostra Aetate*, issued by the Second Vatican Council on 28 October 1965, 'On the Relationship of the Church to Non-Christian Religions' (n. 4), marks an important milestone in the history of Jewish-Christian relations.

Moreover, the step taken by the Council finds its historical setting in circumstances deeply affected by the memory of the persecution and massacre of Jews which took place in Europe just before and during the Second World War.

Although Christianity sprang from Judaism, taking from it certain essential elements of its faith and divine cult, the gap dividing them was deepened more and more, to such an extent that Christian and Jew hardly knew each other.

After two thousand years, too often marked by mutual ignorance and frequent confrontation, the Declaration *Nostra Aetate* provides an opportunity to open or to continue a dialogue with a view to better mutual understanding. Over the past nine years, many steps in this direction have been taken in various countries. As a result, it is easier to distinguish the conditions under which a new relationship between Jews and Christians may be worked out and developed. This seems the right moment to propose, following the guidelines of the Council, some concrete suggestions born of experience, hoping that they will help bring into actual existence in the life of the Church the intentions expressed in the conciliar document.

While referring the reader back to this document, we may simply restate here that the spiritual bonds and historical links binding the Church to Judaism condemn (as opposed to the very spirit of Christianity) all forms of anti-Semitism and discrimination, which in any case the dignity of the human person alone would suffice to condemn. Further still, these links and relationships render obligatory a better mutual understanding and renewed mutual esteem. On the practical level in particular, Christians must therefore strive to acquire a better knowledge of the basic components of the religious tradition of Judaism: they must strive to learn by what essential traits the Jews define themselves in the light of their own religious experience.

With due respect for such matters of principle, we simply propose some first practical applications in different essential areas of the Church's life, with a view to launching or developing sound relations between Catholics and their Jewish brothers.

Dialogue

To tell the truth, such relations as there have been between Jew and Christian have scarcely ever risen above the level of monologue. From now on, real dialogue must be established.

Dialogue presupposes that each side wishes to know the other, and wishes to increase and deepen its knowledge of the other. It constitutes a particularly suitable means of favoring a better mutual knowledge and, especially in the case of dialogue between Jews and Christians, of probing the riches of one's own tradition. Dialogue demands respect for the other as he is; above all, respect for his faith and his religious convictions.

In virtue of her divine mission, and her very nature, the Church must preach Jesus Christ to the world (*Ad Gentes*, 2). Lest the witness of Catholics to Jesus Christ should give offence to Jews, they must take care to live and spread their Christian faith while maintaining the strictest respect for religious liberty, in line with the teaching of the Second Vatican Council (Declaration *Dignitatis Humanae*). They will likewise strive to understand the difficulties which arise for the Jewish soul – rightly imbued with an extremely high, pure notion of the divine transcendence – when faced with the mystery of the incarnate Word.

While it is true that a widespread air of suspicion, inspired by an unfortunate past, is still dominant in this particular area, Christians for their part, will be able to see to what extent the responsibility is theirs and deduce practical conclusions for the future.

In addition to friendly talks, competent people will be encouraged to meet and to study together the many problems deriving from the fundamental convictions of Judaism and of Christianity. In order not to hurt (even involuntarily) those taking part, it will be vital to guarantee, not only tact, but a great openness of spirit and diffidence with respect to one's own prejudices.

In whatever circumstances as shall prove possible and mutually acceptable, one might encourage a common meeting in the presence of God, in prayer and silent meditation, a highly efficacious way of finding that humility, that openness of heart and mind, necessary prerequisites for a deep knowledge of oneself and of others. In particular, that will be done in connection with great causes, such as the struggle for peace and justice.

Liturgy

The existing links between the Christian liturgy and the Jewish liturgy will be borne in mind. The idea of a living community in the service of God, and in the service of men for the love of God, such as it is realized in the liturgy, is just as characteristic of the Jewish liturgy as it is of the Christian one. To improve Jewish-Christian relations, it is important to take cognizance of those common elements of the liturgical life (formulas, feasts, rites, etc.) in which the Bible holds an essential place.

An effort will be made to acquire a better understanding of whatever in the Old Testament retains its own perpetual value (cf. *Dei Verbum*, 14-15), since that has not been cancelled by the later interpretation of the New Testament. Rather, the New Testament brings out the full meaning of the Old, while both Old and New illumine and explain each other (cf. *ibid.*, 16). This is all the more important since liturgical reform is now bringing the text of the Old Testament ever more frequently to the attention of Christians.

When commenting on Biblical texts, emphasis will be laid on the continuity of our faith with that of the earlier Covenant, in the perspective of the promises, without minimizing those elements of Christianity which are original. We believe that those promises were fulfilled with the first coming of Christ. But it is nonetheless true that we still await their perfect fulfilment in His glorious return at the end of time.

With respect to liturgical readings, care will be taken to see that homilies based on them will not distort their meaning, especially when it is a question of passages which seem to show the Jewish people as such in an unfavorable light. Efforts will be made to instruct the Christian people that they will understand the true interpretation of all the texts and their meaning for the contemporary believer.

Commissions entrusted with the task of liturgical translation will pay particular attention to the way in which they express those phrases and passages which Christians, if not well informed, might misunderstand because of prejudice. Obviously, one cannot alter the text of the Bible. The point is that, with a version destined for liturgical use, there should be an overriding preoccupation to bring out explicitly the meaning of a text, while taking scriptural studies into account. (Thus the formula 'the Jews', in St John, sometimes according to the context means 'the leaders of the Jews', or 'the adversaries of Jesus', terms which express better the thought of the Evangelist and avoid appearing to arraign the Jewish people as such. Another example is the use of the words 'Pharisee' and 'Pharisaism', which have taken on a largely pejorative meaning.)

The preceding remarks also apply to the introductions to Biblical readings, to the Prayer of the Faithful, and to commentaries printed in missals used by the laity.

Teaching and education

Although there is still a great deal of work to be done, a better understanding of Judaism itself and its relationship to Christianity has been achieved in recent years thanks to the teaching of the Church, the study and research of scholars, as also to the beginning of dialogue. In this respect, the following facts deserve to be recalled:

It is the same God, 'inspirer and author of the books of both Testaments' (*Dei Verbum*, 16), who speaks both in the old and new Covenants.

Judaism in the time of Christ and the Apostles was a complex reality, embracing many different trends, many spiritual, religious, social, and cultural values.

The Old Testament and the Jewish tradition founded upon it must not be set against the New Testament in such a way that the former seems to constitute a religion of only justice, fear, and legalism, with no appeal to the love of God and neighbour (cf. Dt 6:56; Lv 19:18; Mt 22:34-40).

Jesus was born of the Jewish people, as were His apostles and a large number of His first disciples. When He revealed Himself as the Messiah and Son (cf. Mt 16:16), the bearer of the new Gospel message, He did so as the fulfilment and perfection of the earlier Revelation. And although His teaching had a profoundly new character, Christ, nevertheless, in many instances, took His stand on the teaching of the Old Testament. The New Testament is profoundly marked by its relation to the Old. As the Second Vatican Council declared: 'God, the inspirer and author of the books of both Testaments, wisely arranged that the New Testament be hidden in the Old and the Old be made manifest in the New' (*Dei Verbum*, 16). Jesus also used teaching methods similar to those employed by the rabbis of His time.

With regard to the trial and death of Jesus, the Council recalled that 'what happened in His passion cannot be blamed upon all the Jews then living, without distinction, nor upon the Jews of today' (*Nostra Aetate*).

The history of Judaism did not end with the destruction of Jerusalem, but rather went on to develop a religious tradition. And, although we believe that the importance and meaning of that tradition were deeply affected by the coming of Christ, it is nonetheless rich in religious values.

With the prophets and the apostle Paul, 'the Church awaits the day, known to God alone, on which all peoples will address the Lord in a single voice and serve Him with one accord' (Zeph 3:9) (*Nostra Aetate*).

Information concerning these questions is important at all levels of Christian instruction and education. Among sources of information, special attention should be paid to the following: catechisms and religious textbooks, history books, the mass media (press, radio, movies, television).

The effective use of these means presupposes the thorough formation of instructors and educators in training schools, seminaries, and universities.

Research into the problems bearing on Judaism and Jewish-Christian relations will be encouraged among specialists, particularly in the fields of exegesis, theology, history, and sociology. Higher institutions of Catholic research, in association if possible with other similar Christian institutions and experts, are invited to contribute to the solution of such problems. Wherever possible, chairs of Jewish Studies will be created, and collaboration with Jewish scholars encouraged.

Joint social action

Jewish and Christian tradition, founded on the word of God, is aware of the value of the human person, the image of God. Love of the same God must show itself in effective action for the good of mankind. In the spirit of the prophets, Jews and Christians will work willingly together, seeking social justice and peace at every level – local, national, and international.

At the same time, such collaboration can do much to foster mutual understanding and esteem.

Conclusion

The Second Vatican Council has pointed out the path to follow in promoting deep fellowship between Jews and Christians. But there is still a long road ahead.

The problem of Jewish-Christian relations concerns the Church as such, since it is when 'pondering her own mystery' that she encounters the mystery of Israel. Therefore, even in areas where no Jewish communities exist, this remains an important problem. There is also an ecumenical aspect to the question: the very return of Christians to the sources and origins of their faith, grafted onto the earlier Covenant, helps the search for unity in Christ, the cornerstone.

In this field, the bishops will know what best to do on the pastoral level, within the general disciplinary framework of the Church and in line with the common teaching of her magisterium. For example, they will create some suitable commissions or secretariats on a national or regional level, or appoint some competent person to promote the implementation of the conciliar directives and the suggestions made above.

On 22 October 1974, the Holy Father instituted for the universal Church this Commission for Religious Relations with the Jews, joined to the Secretariat for promoting Christian Unity. This special Commission, created to encourage and foster religious relations between Jews and Catholics – and to do so eventually in collaboration with other Christians – will be, within the limits of its competence, at the service of all interested organisations, providing information for them, and helping them to pursue their task in conformity with the instructions of the Holy See.

Notes on the Correct Way to Present the Jews and Judaism in Preaching and Catechesis in the Roman Catholic Church, June 1985

Preliminary considerations

On 6 March 1982, Pope John Paul II told delegates of episcopal conferences and other experts, meeting in Rome to study relations between the Church and Judaism:

> You yourselves were concerned, during your sessions, with Catholic teaching and catechesis regarding Jews and Judaism. . . We should aim, in this field, that Catholic teaching at its different levels, in catechesis to children and young people, presents Jews and Judaism, not only in an honest and objective manner, free from prejudices and without any offences, but also with full awareness of the heritage common to Jews and Christians.

In this passage, so charged with meaning, the Holy Father plainly drew inspiration from the Council Declaration *Nostra Aetate*, 4, which says:

> All should take pains, then, lest in catechetical instruction and in the preaching of God's Word they teach anything out of harmony with the truth of the Gospel and the spirit of Christ. . . Since the spiritual patrimony common to Christians and Jews is thus so great, this sacred Synod wishes to foster and recommend mutual understanding and respect.

In the same way, the *Guidelines and Suggestions for Implementing the Conciliar Declaration Nostra Aetate* (§4) ends its Chapter III, entitled 'Teaching and Education', which lists a number of practical things to be done, with this recommendation:

> Information concerning these questions is important at all levels of Christian instruction and education. Among sources of information, special attention should be paid to the following:
> — catechisms and religious textbooks;
> — history books;
> — the mass media (press, radio, cinema, television).
>   The effective use of these means presupposes the thorough formation of instructors and educators in training schools, seminaries and universities.

The paragraphs which follow are intended to serve this purpose.

I. Religious teaching and Judaism

1. In *Nostra Aetate* 4, the Council speaks of the 'spiritual bonds linking' Jews and Christians and of the 'great spiritual patrimony' common to both, and it further asserts that 'the Church of Christ acknowledges that, according to the mystery of God's saving design, the beginning of her faith and her election are already found among the patriarchs, Moses and the prophets'.

2. Because of the unique relations that exist between Christianity and Judaism – 'linked together at the very level of their identity' (John Paul II, 6 March 1982) – relations 'founded on the design of the God of the Covenant' (*ibid.*) – the Jews and Judaism should not occupy an occasional and marginal place in catechesis: their presence there is essential and should be organically integrated.

3. This concern for Judaism in Catholic teaching has not merely historical or archeological foundation. As the Holy Father said in the speech already quoted, after he had again mentioned the 'common patrimony' of the Church and Judaism as 'considerable': 'To assess it carefully in itself and with due awareness of the faith and religious life of the Jewish people *as they are professed and practised still today* can greatly help us to understand better certain aspects of the life of the Church' (italics added). It is then a question of pastoral concern for a still living reality closely related to the Church. The Holy Father has stated this permanent reality of the Jewish people in a remarkable theological formula, in his allocution to the Jewish community of West Germany at Mainz, on 17 November 1980: '. . . the people of God of the Old Covenant, which has never been revoked. . .'.

4. Here we should recall the passage in which the *Guidelines and*

Suggestions (I) tried to define the fundamental condition of dialogue: 'respect for the other as he is', knowledge of the 'basic components of the religious tradition of Judaism', and again learning 'by what essential traits the Jews define themselves in the light of their own religious experience' (Introd.).

5. The singular character and the difficulty of Christian teaching about Jews and Judaism lies in this, that it needs to balance a number of pairs of ideas which express the relation between the two economies of the Old and New Testament: Promise and Fulfilment; Continuity and Newness; Singularity and Universality; Uniqueness and Exemplary Nature.

This means that the theologian or the catechist who deals with the subject needs to show in his practice of teaching that: promise and fulfilment throw light on each other; newness lies in a metamorphosis of what was there before; the singularity of the people of the Old Testament is not exclusive and is open, in the divine vision, to a universal extension; the uniqueness of the Jewish people is meant to have the force of an example.

6. Finally, 'work that is of poor quality and lacking in precision would be extremely detrimental' to Judaeo–Christian dialogue (John Paul II, speech of 6 March 1982). But it would be above all detrimental – since we are talking of teaching and education – to Christian identity (*ibid.*).

7. 'In virtue of her divine mission, the Church', which is to be 'the all-embracing means of salvation' in which alone 'the fullness of the means of salvation can be obtained' (*Unit. Red.* 3), 'must of her nature proclaim Jesus Christ to the world' (cf. *Guidelines and Suggestions,* I). Indeed we believe that it is through him that we go to the Father (cf. Jn 14:6) 'and this is eternal life, that they know thee the only true God and Jesus Christ whom thou has sent' (Jn 17:3).

Jesus affirms (Jn 10:16) that 'there shall be one flock and one shepherd'. Church and Judaism cannot then be seen as two parallel ways of salvation and the Church must witness to Christ as the Redeemer for all, 'while maintaining the strictest respect for religious liberty in line with the teaching of the Second Vatican Council (Declaration *Dignitatis Humanae)' (Guidelines and Suggestions,* I).

8. The urgency and importance of precise, objective and rigorously accurate teaching on Judaism for our faithful follows too from the danger of anti-Semitism which is always ready to reappear under different guises. The question is not merely to uproot from among the faithful the remains of anti-Semitism still to be found here and there, but much rather to arouse in them, through educational work, an exact knowledge of the wholly unique 'bond' (*Nostra Aetate,* 4) which joins us as a Church to the Jews and to Judaism. In this way, they would learn to appreciate and love the latter, who have been chosen by God to prepare the coming of Christ and have preserved everything that was progressively revealed and given in the course of that preparation, notwithstanding their difficulty

in recognizing in him their Messiah.

II.   Relations between the Old[1] and New Testament

1. Our aim should be to show the unity of biblical revelation (O.T. and N.T.) and of the divine plan, before speaking of each historical event, so as to stress that particular events have meaning when seen in history as a whole – from creation to fulfilment. this history concerns the whole human race and especially believers. Thus the definitive meaning of the election of Israel does not become clear except in the light of the complete fulfilment (Rom 9-11) and election in Jesus Christ is still better under-stood with reference to the announcement and the promise (cf. Heb 4:1-11).

2. We are dealing with singular happenings which concern a singular nation but are destined, in the sight of God who reveals His purpose, to take on universal and exemplary significance.

The aim is moreover to present the events of the Old Testament not as concerning only the Jews but also as touching us personally. Abraham is truly the father of our faith (cf. Rom 4:11-12; Roman Canon: *patriarchae nostri Abrahae*). And it is said (1 Cor 10:1): '*Our* fathers were all under the cloud, and all passed through the sea.' The patriarchs, prophets and other personalities of the Old Testament have been vener-ated and always will be venerated as saints in the liturgical tradition of the Oriental Church as also of the Latin Church.

3. From the unity of the divine plan derives the problem of the relation between the Old and New Testaments. The Church already from apostolic times (cf. 1 Cor 10:11; Heb 10:1) and then constantly in tradition resolved this problem by means of typology, which emphasizes the primordial value that the Old Testament must have in the Christian view. Typology however makes many people uneasy and is perhaps the sign of a problem unresolved.

4. Hence in using typology, the teaching and practice of which we have received from the liturgy and from the Fathers of the Church, we should be careful to avoid any transition from the Old to the New Testament which might seem merely a rupture. The Church, in the spontaneity of the Spirit which animates her, has vigorously condemned the attitude of Marcion[2] and always opposed his dualism.

---

1 We continue to use the expression *Old Testament* because it is tra⋯⋯ional (cf. already 2 Cor 3:14) but also because 'Old' does not mean 'out of date' or 'out-worn'. In any case, it is the *permanent* value of the OT as a source of Christian revelation that is emphasised here (cf. *Dei Verbum*, 3).

2 A man of gnostic tendency who in the second century rejected the Old Testa-ment and part of the New as the work of an evil god, a demiurge. The Church reacted strongly against this heresy (cf. Irenaeus).

5. It should also be emphasized that typological interpretation consists in reading the Old Testament as preparation and, in certain aspects, outline and foreshadowing of the New (cf., e.g., Heb 5:5-10, etc.). Christ is henceforth the key and point of reference to the Scriptures: 'the rock *was* Christ' (1 Cor 10:4).

6. It is true then, and should be stressed, that the Church and Christians read the Old Testament in the light of the event of the dead and risen Christ and that on these grounds there is a Christian reading of the Old Testament which does not necessarily coincide with the Jewish reading. Thus Christian identity and Jewish identity should be carefully distinguished in their respective reading of the Bible. But this detracts nothing from the value of the Old Testament in the Church and does nothing to hinder Christians from profiting discerningly from the traditions of Jewish reading.

7. Typological reading only manifests the unfathomable riches of the Old Testament, its inexhaustible content and the mystery of which it is full, and should not lead us to forget that it retains its own value as revelation that the New Testament often does no more than resume (cf. Mk 12:29-31). Moreover, the New Testament itself demands to be read in the light of the Old. Primitive Christian catechesis constantly had recourse to this (cf., e.g., 1 Cor 5:6-8; 10:1-11).

8. Typology further signifies reaching toward the accomplishment of the divine plan, when 'God will be all in all' (1 Cor 15:28). This holds true also for the Church which, realized already in Christ, yet awaits its definitive perfecting as the body of Christ. The fact that the body of Christ is still tending toward its full stature (cf. Eph 4:12-19) takes nothing from the value of being a Christian. So also the calling of the patriarchs and the exodus from Egypt do not lose their importance and value in God's design from being at the same time intermediate stages (cf., e.g., *Nostra Aetate*, 4).

9. The exodus, for example, represents an experience of salvation and liberation that is not complete in itself, but has in it, over and above its own meaning, the capacity to be developed further. Salvation and liberation are already accomplished in Christ and gradually realized by the sacraments in the Church. This makes way for the fulfilment of God's design, which awaits its final consummation with the return of Jesus as Messiah, for which we pray each day. The kingdom, for the coming of which we also pray each day, will be finally established. With salvation and liberation the elect and the whole of creation will be transformed in Christ (Rom 8:19-23).

10. Furthermore, in underlining the eschatological dimension of Christianity we shall reach a greater awareness that the people of God of the Old and the New Testament are tending toward a like end in the future: the coming or return of the Messiah – even if they start from

two different points of view. It is more clearly understood that the person of the Messiah is not only a point of division for the people of God but also a point of convergence (cf. *Sussidi per l'ecomenismo* of the diocese of Rome, n. 140). Thus it can be said that Jews and Christians meet in a comparable hope, founded on the same promise made to Abraham (cf. Gen 12:1-3; Heb 6:13-18).

11. Attentive to the same God who has spoken, hanging on the same word, we have to witness to one same memory and one common hope in him who is the master of history. We must also accept our responsibility to prepare the world for the coming of the Messiah by working together for social justice, respect for the rights of persons and nations and for social and international reconciliation. To this we are driven, Jews and Christians, by the command to love our neighbor, by a common hope for the kingdom of God and by the great heritage of the prophets. Transmitted soon enough by catechesis, such a conception would teach young Christians in a practical way to cooperate with Jews, going beyond simple dialogue (cf. *Guidelines*, IV).

III. Jewish roots of Christianity

12. Jesus was and always remained a Jew; his ministry was deliberately limited 'to the lost sheep of the house of Israel' (Mt 15:24). Jesus is fully a man of his time, and of his environment – the Jewish Palestinian one of the first century, the anxieties and hopes of which he shared. This cannot but underline both the reality of the incarnation and the very meaning of the history of salvation, as it has been revealed in the Bible (cf. Rom 1:3-4; Gal 4:4-5).

13. Jesus' relations with Biblical law and its more or less traditional interpretations are undoubtedly complex, and he showed great liberty toward it (cf. the 'antitheses' of the Sermon on the Mount: Mt 5:21-48, bearing in mind the exegetical difficulties – his attitude to rigorous observance of the Sabbath: Mk 3:1-6 , etc.).

But there is no doubt that he wished to submit himself to the law (cf. Gal 4:4), that he was circumcised and presented in the temple like any Jew of his time (cf. Lk 2:21, 22-24), and he was trained in the law's observance. He extolled respect for it (cf. Mt 5: 17-20) and invited obedience to it (cf. Mt 8:4). The rhythm of his life was marked by observance of pilgrimages on great feasts, even from his infancy (cf. Lk 2:41-50; Jn 2:13; 7:10 etc.). The importance of the cycle of the Jewish feasts has been frequently underlined in the Gospel of John (cf. 2:13; 5:1; 7:2;. 10:37; 10:22; 12:1; 13:1; 18:28; 19:42, etc.).

14. It should be noted also that Jesus often taught in the synagogues (cf. Mt 4:23; 9:35; Lk 4:15-18; Jn 18:20, etc.) and in the temple (cf. Jn 18:20, etc.), which he frequented as did the disciples even after the resurrection (cf., e.g., Acts 2:46; 3:1; 21:26, etc.). He wished to put in the

context of synagogue worship the proclamation of his Messiahship (cf. Lk 4:16-21). but above all he wished to achieve the supreme act of the gift of himself in the setting of the domestic liturgy of the Passover, or at least of the paschal festivity (cf. Mk 14:1, 12 and parallels; Jn 18:28). This also allows of a better understanding of the 'memorial' character of the Eucharist.

15. Thus the Son of God is incarnate in a people and a human family (cf. Gal 4:4; Rom 9:5). This takes away nothing, quite the contrary, from the fact that he was born for all men (Jewish shepherds and pagan wise men are found at his crib: Lk 2:8-20; Mt 2:1-12) and died for all men (at the foot of the cross there are Jews, among them Mary and John: Jn 19:25-27, and pagans like the centurion: Mk 15:39 and parallels). Thus he made two peoples one in his flesh (cf. Eph 2:14-17). This explains why with the *Ecclesia ex Gentibus* we have, in Palestine and elsewhere, an *Ecclesia ex circumcisione*, of which Eusebius for example speaks (H.E. IV, 5).

16. His relations with the Pharisees were not always or wholly polemical. Of this there are many proofs: it is Pharisees who warn Jesus of the risks he is running (Lk 13:31); some Pharisees are praised – e.g., 'the scribe' of Mk 12:34; Jesus eats with Pharisees (Lk 7:36; 14:1).

17. Jesus shares, with the majority of Palestinian Jews of that time, some pharisaic doctrines: the resurrection of the body; forms of piety, like almsgiving, prayer, fasting (cf. Mt 6:1-18) and the liturgical practice of addressing God as Father; the priority of the commandment to love God and our neighbour (cf. Mk 12:28-34). This is so also with Paul (cf. Acts 23:8), who always considered his membership of the Pharisees as a title of honour (cf. Acts 23:6, 26:5; Phil 3:5).

18. Paul also, like Jesus himself, used methods of reading and interpreting Scripture and of teaching his disciples which were common to the Pharisees of their time. This applies to the use of parables in Jesus' ministry, as also to the method of Jesus and Paul of supporting a conclusion with a quotation from Scripture.

19. It is noteworthy too that the Pharisees are not mentioned in accounts of the Passion. Gamaliel (Acts 5:34-39) defends the apostles in a meeting of the Sanhedrin. An exclusively negative picture of the Pharisees is likely to be inaccurate and unjust (cf. *Guidelines*, Note 1). If in the Gospels and elsewhere in the New Testament there are all sorts of unfavourable references to the Pharisees, they should be seen against the background of a complex and diversified movement. Criticisms of various types of Pharisees are moreover not lacking in Rabbinical sources (cf. the *Babylon Talmud*, the *Sotah* treatise 22b, etc.). 'Phariseeism' in the pejorative sense can be rife in any religion. It may also be stressed that, if Jesus shows himself severe toward the Pharisees, it is because he is closer to them than to other contemporary Jewish groups (cf. *supra*, n. 17).

20. All this should help us to understand better what St. Paul says (Rom 11:16ff) about the 'root' and the 'branches'. The Church and Christianity, for all their novelty, find their origin in the Jewish milieu of the first century of our era, and more deeply still in the 'design of God' (*Nostra Aetate*, 4), realized in the patriarchs, Moses and the prophets (*ibid.*), down to its consummation in Christ Jesus.

IV. The Jews in the New Testament

21. The *Guidelines* already say (note 1) that 'the formula "the Jews" sometimes, according to the context, means "the leaders of the Jews" or "the adversaries of Jesus", terms which express better the thought of the evangelist and avoid appearing to arraign the Jewish people as such'.

An objective presentation of the role of the Jewish people in the New Testament should take account of these various facts:

A. The Gospels are the outcome of long and complicated editorial work. The dogmatic constitution *Dei Verbum*, following the Pontifical Biblical Commission's Instruction *Sancta Mater Ecclesia*, distinguishes three stages: 'The sacred authors wrote the four Gospels, selecting some things from the many which had been handed on by word of mouth or in writing, reducing some of them to a synthesis, explicating some things in view of the situation of their Churches, and preserving the form of proclamation, but always in such fashion that they told us the honest truth about Jesus' (n. 19).

Hence it cannot be ruled out that some references hostile or less than favourable to the Jews have their historical context in conflicts between the nascent Church and the Jewish community. Certain controversies reflect Christian–Jewish relations long after the time of Jesus.

To establish this is of capital importance if we wish to bring out the meaning of certain Gospel texts for the Christians of today.

All this should be taken into account when preparing catechesis and homilies for the last weeks of Lent and Holy Week (cf. already *Guidelines* II, and now also *Sussidi per l'ecumenismo nella diocesi di Roma*, 1982, 144b).

B. It is clear on the other hand that there were conflicts between Jesus and certain categories of Jews of his time, among them Pharisees, from the beginning of his ministry (cf. Mk 2:1, 24, 3:56 etc.).

C. There is moreover the sad fact that the majority of the Jewish people and its authorities did not believe Jesus – a fact not merely of history but of theological bearing, of which St. Paul tries hard to plumb the meaning (Rom 9-11).

D. This fact, accentuated as the Christian mission developed, especially among the pagans, led inevitably to a rupture between Judaism and the young Church, now irreducibly separated and divergent in faith, and this state of affairs is reflected in the texts of the New Testament and particularly in the Gospels. There is no question of playing down or glossing over this rupture; that could only prejudice the identity of either side. Nevertheless it certainly does not cancel the spiritual 'bond' of which the Council speaks (*Nostra Aetate,* 4) and which we propose to dwell on here.

E. Reflecting on this in the light of Scripture, notably of the chapters cited from the epistle to the Romans, Christians should never forget that the faith is a free gift of God (cf. Rom 9:12) and that we should never judge the consciences of others. St. Paul's exhortation 'do not boast' in your attitude to 'the root' (Rom 11:18) has its full point here.

F. There is no putting the Jews who knew Jesus and did not believe in him, or those who opposed the preaching of the apostles, on the same plane with Jews who came after or those of today. If the responsibility of the former remains a mystery hidden with God (cf. Rom 11:25), the latter are in an entirely different situation. Vatican II in the declaration on Religious Liberty teaches that 'all men are to be immune from coercion. . . in such wise that in matters religious no one is to be forced to act in a manner contrary to his own beliefs, nor. . . restrained from acting in accordance with his own beliefs' (n. 2). This is one of the bases – proclaimed by the Council – on which Judaeo–Christian dialogue rests.

22. The delicate question of responsibility for the death of Christ must be looked at from the standpoint of the conciliar declaration *Nostra Aetate,* 4 and of *Guidelines and Suggestions* (III): 'What happened in (Christ's) passion cannot be blamed upon all the Jews then living without distinction nor upon the Jews of today'. especially since 'authorities of the Jews and those who followed their lead pressed for the death of Christ'. Again, further on: 'Christ in his boundless love freely underwent his passion and death because of the sins of all men, so that all might attain salvation' (*Nostra Aetate,* 4). The *Catechism* of the Council of Trent teaches that Christian sinners are more to blame for the death of Christ than those few Jews who brought it about – they indeed 'knew not what they did' (cf. Lk 23:34) and we know it only too well (Parts 1, caput V, Quaest. XI). In the same way and for the same reason, 'the Jews should not be presented as repudiated or cursed by God, as if such views followed from the holy Scriptures' (*Nostra Aetate,* 4). even though it is true that "the church is the new people of God" (*ibid.*).

V. The liturgy

23. Jews and Christians find in the Bible the very substance of their liturgy: for the proclamation of God's word, response to it, prayer of praise and intercession for the living and the dead, recourse to the divine mercy. The liturgy of the word in its own structure originates in Judaism. The prayer of Hours and other liturgical texts and formularies have their parallels in Judaism as do the very formulas of our most venerable prayers,

among them the Our Father. The eucharistic prayers also draw inspiration from models in the Jewish tradition. As John Paul II said (Allocution of 6 March 1982): '. . . the faith and religious life of the Jewish people, as they are professed and practiced still today, can greatly help us to understand better certain aspects of the life of the church. Such is the case of liturgy. . .'.

24. This is particularly evident in the great feasts of the liturgical year, like the Passover. Christians and Jews celebrate the Passover: the Jews, the historic Passover looking toward the future; the Christians, the Passover accomplished in the death and resurrection of Christ, although still in expectation of the final consummation (cf. *supra*, n. 9). It is still the 'memorial' which comes to us from the Jewish tradition, with a specific content different in each case. On either side, however, there is a like dynamism: for Christians it gives meaning to the eucharistic celebration (cf. the antiphon *O sacrum convivium*), a paschal celebration and as such a making present of the past, but experienced in the expectation of what is to come.

VI. *Judaism and Christianity in history*

25. The history of Israel did not end in A.D. 70 (cf. *Guidelines*, II). It continued, especially in a numerous diaspora which allowed Israel to carry to the whole world a witness – often heroic – of its fidelity to the one God and to 'exalt him in the presence of all the living' (Tobit 13:4), while preserving the memory of the land of their forefathers at the heart of their hope (Passover *Seder*).

Christians are invited to understand this religious attachment which finds its roots in Biblical tradition, without however making their own any particular religious interpretation of this relationship (cf. *Declaration* of the U.S. Conference of Catholic Bishops, 20 November 1975).

The existence of the state of Israel and its political options should be envisaged not in a perspective which is in itself religious, but in their reference to the common principles of international law.

The permanence of Israel (while so many ancient peoples have disappeared without trace) is an historic fact and a sign to be interpreted within God's design. We must in any case rid ourselves of the traditional idea of a people *punished*, preserved as a *living argument* for Christian apologetic. It remains a chosen people, 'the pure olive on which were grafted the branches of the wild olive which are the Gentiles' (John Paul II, 6 March 1982, alluding to Rom 11:17–24). We must remember how much the balance of relations between Jews and Christians over two thousand years has been negative. We must remind ourselves how the permanence of Israel is accompanied by a continuous spiritual fecundity, in the Rabbinical period, in the Middle Ages and in modern times, taking its start from a patrimony which we long shared, so much so that 'the faith and religious life of the Jewish people, as they are professed and practiced still today, can greatly help us to understand better certain aspects of the life of the Church' (John Paul II, 6 March 1982). Catechesis should on the other hand help in understanding the meaning for the Jews of the extermination during the years 1939–1945, and its consequences.

26. Education and catechesis should concern themselves with the problem of racism, still active in different forms of anti- Semitism. The Council presented it thus: 'Moreover, (the Church), mindful of her common patrimony with the Jews and motivated by the Gospel's spiritual love and by no political considerations, deplores the hatred, persecutions and displays of anti-Semitism directed against the Jews at any time and from any source' (*Nostra Aetate*, 4). The *Guidelines* comment: 'The spiritual bonds and historical links binding the Church to Judaism condemn (as opposed to the very spirit of Christianity) all forms of anti-Semitism and discrimination, which in any case the dignity of the human person alone would suffice to condemn' (*Guidelines*, Preamble).

Conclusion

27. Religious teaching, catechesis and preaching should be a preparation not only for objectivity, justice, and tolerance but also for understanding and dialogue. Our two traditions are so related that they cannot ignore each other. Mutual knowledge must be encouraged at every level. There is evident in particular a painful ignorance of the history and traditions of Judaism, of which only negative aspects and often caricature seem to form part of the stock ideas of many Christians.

That is what these notes aim to remedy. This would mean that the Council text and *Guidelines and Suggestions* would be more easily and faithfully put into practice.

Statement by the World Council of Churches, dialogue with people of living faiths and ideologies (DFI), 1982:

Ecumenical considerations on Jewish–Christian dialogue

Historical note

In 1975 the Consultation on the Church and the Jewish People (CCJP) voted to begin the process that has borne fruit in these Ecumenical Considerations on Jewish–Christian Dialogue. The first step was to request preparatory papers from the various regions with experience in Jewish–Christian dialogue. When the Central Committee adopted 'Guidelines on Dialogue' in 1979, work on developing specific suggestions for Jewish–Christian dialogue began and, after a period of drafting and revisions, a draft was presented for comments to the International Jewish Committee on Interreligious Consultations (IJCIC), the CCJP's primary Jewish dialogue partner. After discussion in the DFI Working Group in 1980, a revised draft was circulated among interested persons in the churches and comments solicited. Many and substantial comments and suggestions were received.

When it met in London Colney, England, in June 1981, the CCJP adopted its final revisions and submitted them to the DFI Working Group, which adopted them at its meeting in Bali, Indonesia, on 2 January 1982, having made its own revisions at a few points. On the advice of the February 1982 WCC Executive Committee, various concerned member churches and various members of the CCJP were further consulted in order to revise and re-order the text. The result, 'Ecumenical Considerations on Jewish–Christian Dialogue' was 'received and commended to the churches for study and action' by the Executive Committee of the World Council of Churches at Geneva on 16 July 1982.

1. Preface

1.1 One of the functions of dialogue is to allow participants to describe and witness to their faith in their own terms. This is of primary importance since self-serving descriptions of other peoples' faith are one of the roots of prejudice, stereotyping, and condescension. Listening carefully to the neighbours' self-understanding enables Christians better to obey the commandment not to bear false witness against their neighbours, whether those neighbours be of long-established religious, cultural or ideological traditions or members of new religious groups. It should be recognised by partners in dialogue that any religion or ideology claiming universality, apart from having an understanding of itself, will also have its own interpretations of other religions and ideologies as part of its own self-understanding. Dialogue gives an opportunity for a mutual questioning of the understanding partners have about themselves and others. It is out of a reciprocal willingness to listen and learn that significant dialogue grows (WCC Guidelines on Dialogue, 111.4).

1.2 In giving such guidelines applicable to all dialogues, the World Council of Churches speaks primarily to its member churches as it defines the need for and gifts to be received by dialogue. People of other faiths may choose to define their understanding of dialogue, and their expectations as to how dialogue with Christians may affect their own traditions and attitudes and may lead to a better understanding of Christianity. Fruitful 'mutual questioning of the understanding partners have about themselves and others' requires the spirit of dialogue. But the WCC Guidelines do not predict what partners in dialogue may come to learn about themselves, their history, and their problems. Rather they speak within the churches about faith, attitudes, actions, and problems of Christians.

1.3 In all dialogues distinct asymmetry between any two communities of faith becomes an important fact. Already terms like faith, theology, religion, Scripture, people, etc. are not innocent or neutral. Partners in dialogue may rightly question the very language in which each thinks about religious matters.

1.4 In the case of Jewish–Christian dialogue a specific historical and theological asymmetry is obvious. While an understanding of Judaism in New Testament times becomes an integral and indispensable part of any Christian theology, for Jews, a 'theological' understanding of Christianity is of a less than essential or integral significance. Yet, neither community of faith has developed without awareness of the other.

1.5 The relations between Jews and Christians have unique characteristics because of the ways in which Christianity historically emerged out of Judaism. Christian understandings of that process constitute a necessary part of the dialogue and give urgency to the enterprise. As Christianity came to define its own identity over against Judaism, the Church developed its own understandings, definitions and terms for what it had inherited from Jewish traditions, and for what it read in the Scriptures common to Jews and Christians. In the process of defining its own identity the Church defined Judaism, and assigned to the Jews definite roles in its understanding of God's acts of salvation. It should not be surprising that Jews resent those Christian theologies in which they as a people are assigned to play a negative role. Tragically, such patterns of thought in Christianity have often led to overt acts of condescension, persecutions, and worse.

1.6 Bible-reading and worshipping Christians often believe that they 'know Judaism' since they have the Old Testament, the records of Jesus' debates with Jewish teachers and the early Christian reflections on the Judaism of their times. Furthermore, no other religious tradition has been so thoroughly 'defined' by preachers and teachers in the Church as has Judaism. This attitude is often enforced by lack of knowledge about the history of Jewish life and thought through the 1,900 years since the parting of the ways of Judaism and Christianity.

1.7 For these reasons there is special urgency for Christians to listen, through study and dialogue, to ways in which Jews understand their history and their traditions, their faith and their obedience 'in their own terms'. Furthermore, a mutual listening to how each is perceived by the other may be a step towards understanding the hurt, overcoming the fears, and correcting the misunderstandings that have thrived on isolation.

1.8 Both Judaism and Christianity comprise a wide spectrum of opinions, options, theologies, and styles of life and service. Since generalizations often produce stereotyping, Jewish–Christian dialogue becomes the more significant by aiming at as full as possible a representation of views within the two communities of faith.

2. *Towards a Christian understanding of Jews and Judaism*

2.1 Through dialogue with Jews many Christians have come to appreciate the richness and vitality of Jewish faith and life in the covenant and have been enriched in their own understandings of God and the divine will for all creatures.

2.2 In dialogue with Jews, Christians have learned that the actual history of Jewish faith and experiences does not match the images of Judaism that have dominated a long history of Christian teaching and writing, images that have been spread by Western culture and literature into other parts of the world.

2.3 A classical Christian tradition sees the Church replacing Israel as God's people, and the destruction of the second temple of Jerusalem as a warrant for this claim. The covenant of God with the people of Israel was only a preparation for the coming of Christ, after which it was abrogated.

2.4 Such a theological perspective has had fateful consequences. As the Church replaced the Jews as God's people, the Judaism that survived was seen as a fossilized religion of legalism – a view now perpetuated by scholarship which claims no theological interests. Judaism of the first centuries before and after the birth of Jesus was therefore called 'Late Judaism'. The Pharisees were considered to represent the acme of legalism, Jews and Jewish groups were portrayed as negative models, and the truth and beauty of Christianity were thought to be enhanced by setting up Judaism as false and ugly.

2.5 Through a renewed study of Judaism and in dialogue with Jews, Christians have become aware that Judaism in the time of Christ was in an early stage of its long life. Under the leadership of the Pharisees the Jewish people began a spiritual revival of remarkable power, which gave them the vitality capable of surviving the catastrophe of the loss of the temple. It gave birth to Rabbinic Judaism which produced the Mishnah and Talmud and built the structures for a strong and creative life through the centuries.

2.6 As a Jew, Jesus was born into this tradition. In that setting he was nurtured by the Hebrew Scriptures, which he accepted as authoritative and to which he gave a new interpretation in his life and teaching. In this context Jesus announced that the Kingdom of God was at hand, and in his resurrection his followers found the confirmation of his being both Lord and Messiah.

2.7 Christians should remember that some of the controversies reported in the New Testament between Jesus and the 'scribes and Pharisees' find parallels within Pharisaism itself and its heir, Rabbinic Judaism. These controversies took place in a Jewish context, but when the words of Jesus came to be used by Christians who did not identify with the Jewish people as Jesus did, such sayings often became weapons in anti-Jewish polemics and thereby their original intention was tragically distorted. An internal Christian debate is now taking place on the question of how to understand passages in the New Testament that seem to contain anti-Jewish references.

2.8 Judaism, with its rich history of spiritual life, produced the Talmud as the normative guide for Jewish life in thankful response to the grace of God's covenant with the people of Israel. Over the centuries important commentaries, profound philosophical works and poetry of spiritual depth have been added. For Judaism the Talmud is central and authoritative. Judaism is more than the religion of the Scriptures of Israel. What Christians call the Old Testament has received in the Talmud and later writings interpretations that for Jewish tradition share in the authority of Moses.

2.9 For Christians the Bible with the two Testaments is also followed by traditions of interpretation, from the Church Fathers to the present time. Both Jews and Christians live in the continuity of their Scripture and Tradition.

2.10 Christians as well as Jews look to the Hebrew Bible as the story recording Israel's sacred memory of God's election and covenant with this people. For Jews, it is their own story in historical continuity with the present. Christians, mostly of gentile background since early in the life of the Church, believe themselves to be heirs to this same story by grace in Jesus Christ. The relationship between the two communities, both worshipping the God of Abraham, Isaac and Jacob, is a given historical fact, but how it is to be understood theologically is a matter of internal discussion among Christians, a discussion than can be enriched by dialogue with Jews.

2.11 Both commonalities and differences between the two faiths need to be examined carefully. Finding in the Scriptures of the Old and New Testaments the authority sufficient for salvation, the Christian Church shares Israel's faith in the One God, whom it knows in the Spirit as the God and Father of the Lord Jesus Christ. For Christians, Jesus Christ is the only begotten Son of the Father, through whom millions have come to share in the love of, and to adore, the God who first made covenant with the people of Israel. Knowing the One God in Jesus Christ through the Spirit, therefore, Christians worship that God with a Trinitarian confession to the One God, the God of Creation, Incarnation and Pentecost. In so doing, the Church worships in a language foreign to

Jewish worship and sensitivities, yet full of meaning to Christians.

2.12 Christians and Jews both believe that God has created men and women as the crown of creation and has called them to be holy and to exercise stewardship over the creation in accountability to God. Jews and Christians are taught by their Scriptures and Traditions to know themselves responsible to their neighbours especially to those who are weak, poor and oppressed. In various and distinct ways they look for the day in which God will redeem the creation. In dialogue with Jews many Christians come to a more profound appreciation of the Exodus hope of liberation, and pray and work for the coming of righteousness and peace on earth.

2.13 Christians learn through dialogue with Jews that for Judaism the survival of the Jewish people is inseparable from its obedience to God and God's covenant.

2.14 During long periods, both before and after the emergence of Christianity, Jews found ways of living in obedience to Torah, maintaining and deepening their calling as a peculiar people in the midst of the nations. Through history there are times and places in which Jews were allowed to live, respected and accepted by the cultures in which they resided, and where their own culture thrived and made a distinct and sought-after contribution to their Christian and Muslim neighbours. Often lands not dominated by Christians proved most favourable for Jewish diaspora living. There were even times when Jewish thinkers came to 'make a virtue out of necessity' and considered diaspora living to be the distinct genius of Jewish existence.

2.15 Yet, there was no time in which the memory of the Land of Israel and of Zion, the city of Jerusalem, was not central in the worship and hope of the Jewish people. 'Next year in Jerusalem' was always part of Jewish worship in the diaspora. And the continued presence of Jews in the Land and in Jerusalem was always more than just one place of residence among all the others.

2.16 Jews differ in their interpretations of the State of Israel, as to its religious and secular meaning. It constitutes for them part of the long search for that survival which has always been central to Judaism through the ages. Now the quest for statehood by Palestinians – Christian and Muslim – as part of their search for survival as a people in the Land – also calls for full attention.

2.17 Jews, Christians and Muslims have all maintained a presence in the Land from their beginnings. While 'the Holy Land' is primarily a Christian designation, the Land is holy to all three. Although they may understand its holiness in different ways, it cannot be said to be 'more holy' to one than to another.

2.18 The need for dialogue is the more urgent when under strain the dialogue is tested. Is it mere debate and negotiation or is it grounded in faith that God's will for the world is secure peace with justice and compassion?

3. Hatred and persecution of Jews – a continuing concern

3.1 Christians cannot enter into dialogue with Jews without the awareness that hatred and persecution of Jews have a long persistent history, especially in countries where Jews constitute a minority among Christians. The tragic history of the persecution of Jews includes massacres in Europe and the Middle East by the Crusaders, the Inquisition, pogroms, and the Holocaust. The World Council of Churches Assembly at its first meeting in Amsterdam, 1948, declared: 'We call upon the churches we represent to denounce anti-Semitism, no matter what its origin, as absolutely irreconcilable with the profession and practice of the Christian faith. Anti-Semitism is sin against God and man'. This appeal has been reiterated many times. Those who live where there is a record of acts of hatred against Jews can serve the whole church by unmasking the ever-present danger they have come to recognize.

3.2 Teachings of contempt for Jews and Judaism in certain Christian traditions proved a spawning ground for the evil of the Nazi Holocaust. The church must learn so to preach and teach the Gospel as to make sure that it cannot be used towards contempt for Judaism and against the Jewish people. A further response to the Holocaust by Christians, and one which is shared by their Jewish partners, is a resolve that it will never happen again to the Jews or to any other people.

3.3 Discrimination against and persecution of Jews have deep-rooted socio-economic and political aspects. Religious differences are magnified to justify ethnic hatred in support of vested interests. Similar phenomena are also evident in many interracial conflicts. Christians should oppose all such religious prejudices, whereby people are made scapegoats for the failures and problems of societies and political regimes.

3.4 Christians in parts of the world with a history of little or no persecution of Jews do not wish to be conditioned by the specific experiences of justified guilt among other Christians. Rather, they explore in their own ways the significance of Jewish-Christian relations, from the earliest times to the present, for their life and witness.

4. Authentic Christian witness

4.1 Christians are called to witness to their faith in word and deed. The Church has a mission and it cannot be otherwise. This mission is not one of choice.

4.2 Christians have often distorted their witness by coercive proselytism – conscious and unconscious, overt and subtle. Referring to proselytism between Christian churches, the Joint Working Group of the Roman Catholic Church and the World Council of Churches stated: 'Proselytism embraces whatever violates the right of the human person, Christian or non-Christian, to be free from external coercion in religious matters' (*Ecumenical Review*, 1/1971, p. 11).

4.3 Such rejection of proselytism, and such advocacy of respect for the integrity and the identity of all persons and all communities of faith are urgent in relation to Jews, especially those who live as minorities among Christians. Steps towards assuring non-coercive practices are of highest importance. In dialogue ways should be found for the exchange of concerns, perceptions, and safeguards in these matters.

4.4 While Christians agree that there can be no place for coercion of any kind, they do disagree – on the basis of their understandings of the Scriptures – as to what constitutes authentic forms of mission. There is a wide spectrum, from those who see the very presence of the Church in the world as the witness called for, to those who see mission as the explicit and organised proclamation of the gospel to all who have not accepted Jesus as their Saviour.

4.5 This spectrum as to mission in general is represented in the different views of what is authentic mission to Jews. Here some of the specifics are as follows: There are Christians who view a mission to the Jews as having a very special salvific significance, and those who believe the conversion of the Jews to be the eschatological event that will climax the history of the world. There are those who would place no special emphasis on a mission to the Jews, but would include them in the one mission to all those who have not accepted Christ as their Saviour. There are those who believe that a mission to the Jews is not part of an authentic Christian witness, since the Jewish people finds its fulfilment in faithfulness to God's covenant of old.

4.6 Dialogue can rightly be described as a mutual witness, but only when the intention is to hear the others in order better to understand their faith, hopes, insights, and concerns, and to give, to the best of one's ability one's own understanding of one's own faith. The spirit of dialogue is to be fully present to one another in full openness and human vulnerability.

4.7 According to Rabbinic law, Jews who confess Jesus as the Messiah are considered apostate Jews. but for many Christians of Jewish origin, their identification with the Jewish people is a deep spiritual reality to which they seek to give expression in various ways, some by observing parts of Jewish tradition in worship and life style, many by a special commitment to the well-being of the Jewish people and to a peaceful and secure future for the State of Israel. Among Christians of Jewish origin there is the same wide spectrum of attitudes towards mission as among other Christians, and the same criteria for dialogue and against coercion apply.

4.8 As Christians of different traditions enter into dialogue with Jews in local, national, and international situations, they will come to express their understanding of Judaism in other language, style, and ways than has been done in these Ecumenical Considerations. Such understandings are to be shared among the churches for enrichment of all.

BIBLIOGRAPHY

M. Barth, *Jesus the Jew*, Atlanta, 1978.

G. Baum, *Jews and the Gospels*, London, 1961.

— —, *Christian Theology after Auschwitz*, London, 1976.

A. Bea, *The Church and the Jewish People*, New York, 1966.

T. E. Bird (ed.), *Modern Theologians: Christians and Jews*, London, 1967.

C. H. Bishop, *How Catholics look at Jews*, New York, 1974.

B. Z. Bokser, *Judaism and the Christian Predicament*, New York, 1967.

E. Borowitz, *Contemporary Christologies: A Jewish Response*, New York, 1980.

A. A. Cohen, *The Myth of the Judeo-Christian Tradition*, New York, 1971.

A. A. Cohen and P. Mendes Flohr (eds.), *Contemporary Jewish Religious Thought*, New York, 1987.

H. Croner (ed.), *Stepping Stones to Jewish–Christian Relations*, New York, 1977.

— —, (ed.), *More Stepping Stones to Jewish–Christian Relations*, New York, 1985.

H. Croner and L. Klenicki (eds.), *Issues in the Jewish–Christian Dialogue: Jewish Perspectives on Covenant, Mission and Witness*, New York, 1979.

A. T. Davies (ed.), *Anti-Semitism and the Christian Mind*, New York, 1969.

— —, (ed.), *Anti-Semitism and the Foundations of Christianity*, New York, 1979.

A. R. Eckardt, *Elder and Younger Brothers*, New York, 1973.

— —, *Your People, My People*, New York, 1974.

— —, *Long Night's Journey into Day: Life and Faith after the Holocaust*, Detroit, 1982.

— —, *Jews and Christians*, Bloomington, 1986.

E. Fisher, *Faith without Prejudice*, New York, 1977.

— —, *Seminary Education and Christian–Jewish Relations*, Washington, 1983.

E. Fisher, A. J. Rudin, and M. H. Tanenbaum (eds.), *Twenty Years of Jewish–Catholic Relations*, New York, 1986.

E. H. Flannery, *The Anguish of the Jews*, New York, 1985.

E. Fleischner, *Judaism in German Christian Theology since 1945*, Metuchen, NJ, 1975.

— —, (ed.), *Auschwitz, Beginning of a New Era?*, New York, 1977.

A. Gilbert, *The Vatican Council and the Jews*, New York, 1968.

F. Heer, *God's First Love*, New York, 1967.

M. T. Hoch and B. Dupuy, *Les Eglises devant le Judaïsme*, Paris, 1980.

J. Isaac, *The Teaching of Contempt*, New York, 1964.

— —, *Jesus and Israel*, New York, 1971.

W. Jacob, *Christianity through Jewish Eyes*, Cincinnati, 1974.

C. Klein, *Anti-Judaism in Christian Theology*, London, 1978.

L. Klenicki and G. Wigoder (eds.), *A Dictionary of the Jewish–Christian Dialogue*, New York, 1984.

H. Küng and W. Hasper (eds.), *Christians and Jews*, New York, 1974.

F. H. Littell, *The Crucifixion of the Jews*, New York, 1975.

M. B. McGarry, *Christology after Auschwitz*, New York, 1977.

Y. Malachy, *American Fundamentalism and Israel*, Jerusalem, 1978.

M. Mendes, *The Vatican and Israel* (Hebrew), Jerusalem, 1983.

F. Mussner, *Tractate on the Jews*, Philadelphia and London, 1984.

P. Opsahl and M. Tanenbaum (eds.), *Speaking of God Today: Jews and Lutherans in Conversation*, New York, 1974.

J. Parkes, *The Conflict of the Church and the Synagogue* (London, 1934), New York, 1961.

— —, *Prelude to Dialogue*, London, 1969.

J. Pawlikowski, *Catechetics and Prejudice*, New York, 1973.

— —, *What are they saying about Jewish–Christian Relations?* New York, 1980.

— —, *Christ in the Light of the Christian–Jewish Dialogue*, New York, 1982.

A. Peck (ed.), *Jews and Christians after the Holocaust*, Philadelphia, 1982.

M. Pragai, *Faith and Fulfilment*, London, 1985.

S. E. Rosenberg, *The Christian Problem: A Jewish View*, New York, 1986.

R. Ruether, *Faith and Fratricide*, New York, 1974.

E. P. Sanders, *Paul and Palestinian Judaism*, New York, 1977.

S. Sandmel, *We Jews and Jesus*, New York, 1965.

— —, *We Jews and You Christians*, New York, 1967.

K. Stendahl, *Paul among the Jews and Gentiles*, New York, 1976.

F. E. Talmadge (ed.), *Disputation and Dialogue*, New York, 1975.

M. Tanenbaum, M. Wilson, J. Rudin (eds.), *Evangelicals and Jews in Conversation*, Grand Rapids, 1978.

C. Thoma, *A Christian Theology of Judaism*, New York, 1980.

P. Van Buren, *Discerning the Way*, New York, 1980.

— —, *A Christian Theology of the People, Israel*, New York, 1983.

Bibliography

Journals

Face to Face (New York)
Immanuel (Jerusalem)
Jewish–Christian Relations (formerly *Christian Attitudes on Jews and Judaism*) (London)
Journal of Ecumenical Studies (Philadelphia)
Judaism (New York)

INDEX